FOOLPROOF

FREEZER

·   *   ·

FOOLPROOF ❄ FREEZER

60 FUSS-FREE DISHES THAT MAKE
THE MOST OF YOUR FREEZER

REBECCA WOODS

PHOTOGRAPHY BY
RITA PLATTS

Hardie Grant

QUADRILLE

Many thanks to everyone who helped me write this book: Stacey for signing me up, Rita for the beautiful photography, Louie for gorgeous props, Alicia for design, and Valeria, George and Sophie for excellent help in the kitchen – and to all my friends and family who were willing guinea pigs during recipe testing.

Publishing Director
Sarah Lavelle

Editor
Stacey Cleworth

Editorial Assistant
Sofie Shearman

Series Designer
Emily Lapworth

Designer
Alicia House

Photographer
Rita Platts

Food Stylist
Rebecca Woods

Prop Stylist
Louie Waller

Head of Production
Stephen Lang

Production Controller
Sabeena Atchia

First published in 2021 by Quadrille,.
an imprint of Hardie Grant Publishing

Quadrille
52–54 Southwark Street
London SE1 1UN
quadrille.com

Text © Quadrille 2021
Photography © Rita Platts 2021
Design and layout © Quadrille 2021

Cataloguing in Publication Data: a catalogue record for this book is available from the British Library.

9781787136595

Printed in China

FSC
www.fsc.org

MIX
Paper from
responsible sources
FSC™ C020056

CONTENTS

INTRODUCTION

In an odd twist of fate, this book came along at perhaps the most opportune time. As the Covid-19 pandemic swept the globe, attentions necessarily turned towards ways to feed ourselves with as little exploration into the outside world as possible. As supermarket shelves emptied, queues lengthened and online delivery slots became like gold dust, I found myself looking to my freezer: to those neglected bags of frozen foods, long since bought and forgotten. With a bit of imagination, I found my freezer detritus – half a bag of hash browns; 'emergency' bread, now complete with freezer burn; a bag of pastries, bought only to provide long-ago house guests with a delicious brekkie; something once alive but now unrecognizable, entombed in a thick layer of ice – could offer a surprisingly appealing alternative to donning a hazmat suit and braving the shops.

The way I see it, the things you find in the freezer fall into five rough categories: meat; fish; the ubiquitous bags of frozen veg; likewise various frozen fruit; and everything else, primarily carbohydrates – pastries, bread, potatoes, etc. These are the building blocks of making exciting fresh food from things you probably already have. Not included here are frozen ready meals or suspicious breaded items moulded into the shape of dinosaurs; buying and cooking with frozen food does not have to mean an over-reliance on unhealthy,

highly-processed items. Although space can generally be found in the freezer for a tub of really good vanilla ice cream, and that token childhood staple, potato waffles, obviously.

But these are things you buy frozen. If we're really going to make good use of our freezers, it helps to have a few homemade sauces and seasonings stashed away too. From a basic pesto, seasoned butters that can add a punch of flavour in an instant, or a homemade chocolate sauce – free from the nasties in processed dessert syrups – great dishes can be made, and all conveniently freeze really well (see page 11 for recipes).

This book is nowhere near exhaustive. There are exciting new freezer products coming on to the market all of the time – the fact that you can now buy bags of frozen avocado and pomegranate seeds was a revelation to me during the writing of this book. I couldn't possibly hope to touch on everything, nor even to show a variety of uses for all these products. However, I have offered alternatives for other freezer ingredients you could sub in, where possible, to keep things a bit more flexible.

My hope is that this book will help shake off the stigma of shopping primarily from the freezer aisle and provide some inspiration, illustrating what a huge range of wholesome dishes can be made from pretty humble ingredients.

FREEZER ESSENTIALS

The chapters in this book are arranged according to my five basic freezer categories:

Meat

There's a huge array of meats available in the frozen aisle in supermarkets, and I have tried to use those for the recipes in this book. But there's no need to stick to these. Most meats freeze really well, and some are even improved by freezing – there's much written about the tenderizing action of freezing on beef steak. Also, many fresh meats are better quality than those you might buy frozen, so you can choose according to how flush you feel at the time. If going fresh, my advice would be to grab what you can while it's on offer and freeze for when the urge to cook takes you. But when cooking with any large cut of meat, make sure you leave enough time for it to defrost naturally before you start cooking. Here are some of my favourite staples:

Smoked bacon lardons are a brilliant freezer staple. They are small, so can be cooked from frozen, and a handful of these can add instant flavour to soups, stews and pasta sauces.

Ham end chunks can often be bought from your butcher or in tubs from the deli counter at the supermarket. These are great for chucking into dishes (such as my Hash Brown & Ham Hash – see page 69) to bulk them up and add protein without too much planning.

Mince is the classic frozen meat, so many of the recipes in this book use varying types of it – lamb, beef, pork, etc. It's economic, quick and easy to use, and once you have cooked it into a dish, it tends to re-freeze well too.

Fish

You can find a massive range of fish in the freezer section, and some of it is fresher and more nutritious than that on the fishmonger's counter as it has been frozen at sea, almost immediately after being caught. This freshness is especially important for dishes such as my Seabass Ceviche on page 44, where the fish is 'cooked' only in the acid from the citrus fruit. However, many frozen fish products come in highly processed formats – when something has been crumbed or battered by the manufacturer, suspicious ingredients tend to sneak in. (And if you have a bag of fresh crumbs in your freezer – see opposite – this is an easy step to do yourself.) Instead, focus on economical plain fish fillets that can be cooked in a huge variety of ways, or the seafood that is often prohibitively expensive to buy fresh, but which you can get great deals on if purchased frozen – think huge prawns, scallops, squid and tuna steaks. If you have an international supermarket near you, the selection is often even broader and you can find all sorts of fish not necessarily found in UK supermarkets, as well as shellfish and baby octopus. Or, of course, buy whatever is on offer fresh and freeze for another day.

Carbs

Pastry can be the base for so many meals or treats – pies, empanadas, fruit tarts, etc. It's easy to combine with many things that you'll find in the freezer, so if you're well stocked, you'll be able to make something, even if the cupboards and fridge are bare.

Bread is also one of the things I use my freezer for a lot. Bread is not pleasant once it starts to go stale, and so every fresh loaf is sliced and placed in a freezer bag, ready to pull out a slice whenever I fancy a piece of toast. And once defrosted, it's as fresh as the day it was frozen. If it is a little past it, see my French Toast recipe on page 70.

If you have bread that's starting to go a little stale, breadcrumbs are a brilliant thing to have stashed in the freezer. They can add a crunch to the top of so many dishes.

Potatoes in various formats seem to take up an enormous amount of space in freezer aisles these days. Arguably, they shouldn't form part of a daily diet, but for a weekend treat, they are a handy way to add a dish to the table with minimal fuss. And there are many ways to make them a little less beige… see my recipes for Patatas Bravas using roasties on page 81, or the Loaded Lattice Fries on page 78.

Vegetables

Where once the frozen veg selection was limited to basics such as peas and sweetcorn kernels, now you can even buy bags of avocado, pomegranate seeds or different mixes for smoothies or stir fries. I'm not going to dwell on these mixes in this book, as no one really needs a recipe for a stir fry or a smoothie. Instead, my recipes try to use just one or several items that you can keep in your freezer and that can be made with other simple ingredients you will likely already have at home.

Freezing veggies is one of the best ways to preserve their nutrients. Anything that is picked and frozen within hours is far more likely to be fresher and more vitamin packed than that wilting veg that has been lurking in the salad box for a fortnight. However, I do need to add a note of caution when cooking with frozen veg: you do have to be quite careful about what you can use it for. Carrots that have been frozen and defrosted will never be crisp enough to add to a lovely Asian-style salad with satisfying results. They will be more mushy as the freezing process starts to break down their cells. However, for cooking with, when you will be heating them and breaking down the cells in that way anyway, they are often as good as fresh. Likewise, greens which have been frozen only need minimal cooking upon defrosting – you certainly don't need to cook them for as long as the same unfrozen variety.

Fruit

Frozen fruit does not share this problem with veg; fruit that has been defrosted and turned a little mushy is not unappealing, making it a star player in your freezer. Chuck a handful of berries, cherries or chunks of tropical fruit into porridge, ice cream, or even into bakes, throw on top of cheesecake or meringue, or blend into a cocktail (see page 140) or smoothie.

Other

There are a few supporting stars that I keep in the freezer, which can add flavour in an instant.

Hardy herbs like thyme and rosemary are a saviour. They freeze well and will hang around in your freezer for indefinite periods of time. Plus, they are so aggressive, any friends that grow them will be desperate to get rid of a few branches that you can stash away.

Soft herbs are available to buy frozen, chopped and in bags or boxes. But you can do this yourself too, if you have an ice cube tray. Simply chop the herbs up and fill the holes of the tray about three-quarters full. Top them up with water and freeze. Once frozen, you can pop the cubes out of the tray and put them in a bag, labelled with what herb they are. This method is great for preserving herbs when you have a large bunch that you don't need to use right away, but it does slightly limit their use. Frozen herb cubes are great for popping into a sauce, stew or soup, but because they do break down, sometimes there is no substitute for fresh, so you will find mentions of fresh herbs in this book, too.

Miso paste can be frozen in small single-serving pots, ready to pop into delicious broths for an intensely savoury umami hit.

Wine left in the bottle at the end of an evening can be put to good use in cooking. Simply use it to top up the holes of an ice cube tray and freeze, then, once frozen, transfer to a bag. With this, it doesn't really matter if you mix and match your wines (but keep white and red wines separate) – just make wine cubes from any dregs and add to the collection in the freezer. They are great for chucking into sauces or risottos, for example, to save you opening a bottle.

Pesto freezes brilliantly, the oil preserving the delicate basil. Make a batch (see opposite) or buy a good quality fresh one, and freeze divided up into smaller portions.

Harissa can be used to add flavour to meats, fish, sauces, dressings, or anything you feel you want to add a little zing to. It's also often sold in rather large cans that can fester at the back of the fridge when forgotten about. Instead, put any leftovers straight in the freezer in tiny freezer boxes, or freeze in ice cube trays.

Curry pastes freeze well if you have leftovers from a fresh tub or jar. Or if you're making it fresh, make extra and store convenient 2–3-tablespoon portions in small tubs in the freezer.

Parmesan rinds can be stashed in freezer bags when you get to the end of the chunk and used to add flavour to soups and stews. See my recipe for Ribbolita on page 82.

Flavoured butters are one of my favourite things to keep in the freezer. They last indefinitely and can be flavoured with whatever you fancy – although do think about how you might practically use that flavour in future when cooking up your creations! My favourites are lemon and herb butter, which can be added to fish and vegetables, and smoked anchovy butter, which is great added to fried beef and lamb steaks. Simply keep a roll in the freezer, and cut off a slice to use whenever a flavour hit is required. (See opposite for recipes.)

Sweet sauces, especially those packaged in plastic squeezy bottles and claiming to be some sort or ice cream or dessert topping, are often highly processed and unhealthy. Instead, I make my own sweet sauces that can be used to add interest to ice cream or make desserts. Various berries and other fruits can be cooked down into compotes, which will freeze well and can be quickly defrosted in the microwave. I also make a chocolate sauce, with good-quality chocolate and much less sugar, which can be used to drizzle over puddings, or as a base for other puddings, such as my chocolate mousse on page 133.

Pantry

Of course, while the freezer can be the source of primary ingredients, keeping your cupboards well stocked will make it far easier to make the most of those freezer ingredients. Keep a good selection of ground spices and dried herbs, and you can add flavour to those frozen meats, fish and veg in an instant. Cans of chopped tomatoes, chickpeas and beans, along with store-cupboard standards rice, pasta, grains (such as barley), lentils, polenta and flour mean the base of a satisfying dish. It's also useful to have eggs, milk and perhaps cream or crème fraîche in the fridge and lemons and onions in the veg rack.

Freezer Feasts

Some of the recipes in this book (those which are pictured on the chapter opener pages) have been labelled as a 'Freezer Feast'. This means that they are great for feeding a crowd from things you might find in a well-stocked freezer. They are a way to impress, and use a high proportion of frozen goods.

Freezer Essential Recipes

Pesto Genovese

Makes about 200g (7oz)

25g (1oz) pine nuts
2 garlic cloves, roughly chopped
75g (2½oz) basil leaves
20g (⅔oz) Parmesan, grated
5 tbsp extra virgin olive oil
sea salt and ground black pepper

Toast the pine nuts in a dry frying pan for a few minutes, then allow to cool.

Tip the pine nuts into the small bowl of a food processor along with the garlic and blitz until roughly chopped. Add the basil and grated Parmesan and blitz again until all chopped and blended.

With the motor still running, trickle in the olive oil until all incorporated. Season to taste with plenty of salt and pepper.

Flavoured Butters

Both make about 250g (9oz)

Lemon and herb butter
200g (7oz) salted butter, softened
finely grated zest of 2 lemons

2 tbsp lemon juice
50g (1¾oz) chopped green herbs
    (or frozen equivalents)

Smoked anchovy butter
200g (7oz) smoked butter, softened
2 × 50g (1¾oz) cans anchovies in olive
    oil, drained
a squeeze of lemon juice
a few good pinches of coarsely ground
    black pepper

To make the butters, combine all the ingredients for your chosen flavour in a bowl and beat together well. Lay out a piece of greaseproof (waxed) paper and spread the butter down one side in a long line. Roll it up and twist the ends of the paper to seal like a cracker.

Place in the fridge to cool down, after which you will be able to shape it into a neater log. Once happy with the shape, pop it in the freezer to slice chunks off when needed. It will keep for months in there.

Chocolate Sauce

Makes about 200g (7oz)

150g (5½oz) dark chocolate
    (70% cocoa solids)
50g (1¾oz) caster (superfine) sugar

Put the chocolate in a saucepan and add the sugar and 75ml (2½fl oz/ 5 tbsp) boiling water. Cook over a low heat for a few minutes until the chocolate has melted and the sauce has thickened. Allow to cool.

Key

Vegetarian (V), vegan (VE) and pescatarian (P) recipes have been marked as such. Additional recipes could be adapted so that they are suitable for vegetarians by simply swapping specific ingredients for an alternative.

MEAT

If you're a committed carnivore, there's sure to be something in this chapter for you. For the traditionalists, there are Little Shepherd's Pies or the hearty Beef & Fennel Casserole with Dumplings. You'll find snacks packed with flavour, such as Smoky & Spicy Buttermilk Drummers, BBQ Beef Empanadas or Lebanese Lamb Flatbreads and winter warmers like the Sausage and Sweet Potato Stew or Moroccan Chicken & Cauliflower Traybake. But for a true meat feast, turn straight to the Chicken Cassoulet for a serving of classic French fare.

SLOW-COOKED BBQ BEEF EMPANADAS

If you have a few friends coming over for drinks, these are a crowd pleaser par excellence, and are also pretty economical. The sauce takes a while to cook, but it's not very involved once it's in the oven. And once they are assembled, you can freeze them unbaked and just pull them out from the freezer to cook from frozen.

2 tbsp olive oil
500g (1lb 2oz) frozen casserole, stewing or braising beef, defrosted
200g (7oz) frozen diced onion (or 1 onion, finely diced)
1 tbsp chopped frozen garlic (or 2 fresh cloves, finely chopped)
2 tsp dried ancho chilli flakes
1 tsp English mustard powder
1 tbsp sweet smoked paprika
5 tbsp cider vinegar
200g (7oz/scant 1 cup) tomato ketchup
1½ tbsp Worcestershire sauce
3 tbsp black treacle or molasses
a few sprays of liquid smoke, to taste (optional but recommended)
plain (all-purpose) flour, for dusting
500g (1lb 2oz) pack shortcrust pastry, defrosted
1 egg, beaten
sea salt and ground black pepper

Will it re-freeze?

Freeze the pastries once assembled and they can be cooked directly from the freezer. You will need to give them about 10 minutes longer in the oven at the same temperature as in the main recipe.

Makes 12
–
Prep 40 mins
–
Cook 2½ hours

Preheat the oven to 140°C/275°F/gas mark 1.

Heat the oil in a heavy-based ovenproof pan over a high heat and fry the beef until browning (you may want to do this in two batches, using half the oil for each batch, as the meat will brown better). Remove from the pan and set aside. Turn the heat down to low–medium and add the onion to the pan. Cook for about 8 minutes, or until softened and translucent, then add the garlic, chilli flakes, mustard powder and paprika and cook for a couple more minutes.

Add the vinegar and stir around to clean the pan, then add the ketchup, Worcestershire sauce, treacle and a few sprays of liquid smoke, if you have it. Stir in 4 tbsp water, season with salt and pepper and stir everything together well. Keep heating gently on the stove until the liquid is hot, then pop a lid on the pan and transfer it to the preheated oven. Cook for about 2 hours until most of the liquid has gone (but you still have a little thick sauce) and the meat is moist and meltingly tender. Stir a couple of times during cooking to check it's not catching on the pan, and if it is starting to, add a splash more water. Once cooked, check the seasoning, then leave to cool completely. You can cook the beef a day or two in advance if you'd like.

Preheat the oven to 190°C/375°F/gas mark 5 and line a large baking sheet with baking parchment.

On a lightly floured surface, roll out the pastry to about 3mm (⅛in) thick. Use a 12cm (4½in) diameter cookie cutter to stamp out circles, getting them as close to each other as you can to make more empanadas. Spoon about 1½ tbsp of the beef filling onto one side of a pastry disc. Brush the edge of the disc with the beaten egg, then fold the bare side of the pastry over the filling and crimp the edges to seal in a half moon shape. Repeat until you have filled all the pastry discs, then brush the tops of them all with the beaten egg to glaze. Transfer the empanadas to the prepared baking sheet and pierce a small hole in the top of each one to allow the steam to escape. Bake the pastries for about 30 minutes, or until the pastry is risen and golden and the filling is piping hot.

This super quick supper is a great way to add flavour to frozen minced beef. If you can get frozen long-stem broccoli, it's well worth it, but otherwise, standard frozen florets will work just fine.

500g (1lb 2oz) frozen Tenderstem
    broccoli or standard florets
3 tbsp sesame seeds
2 tbsp toasted sesame oil
1 tbsp vegetable oil
400g (14oz) frozen minced (ground)
    beef, defrosted
2 tbsp frozen chopped garlic (or 3 fresh
    cloves, finely chopped)
2 tbsp frozen (or fresh) chopped ginger
10–12 spring onions (scallions), whites
    thickly sliced, greens finely sliced
6 tbsp dark soy sauce
2 tbsp honey
1 tbsp Chinese five-spice powder
ground black pepper
cooked jasmine or basmati rice,
    to serve

Freezer adaptation:

You don't have to use broccoli for this
– you could use other fairly large green
freezer veg, such as French beans or
small Brussels sprouts.

Will it re-freeze?

Yes, although the broccoli will be
on the soft side once it's defrosted.
Reheat gently in the microwave.

Put the broccoli in a bowl and cover with warm water to defrost it gently. Drain and set aside to dry. Slice the Tenderstem into long lengths or halve any large florets.

Toast the sesame seeds in a dry frying pan until golden. Remove from the pan and set aside.

Heat the sesame and vegetable oils in a wok or sauté pan over a medium–high heat and add the beef. Cook for a few minutes until the beef is browned, then add the garlic, ginger and the whites of the spring onions and fry for a couple more minutes.

While the beef is cooking, combine the soy sauce, honey and five-spice powder in a small bowl. Tip half of it into the pan and cook for a couple of minutes until the meat is looking glossy. Add the cooked broccoli to the pan with most of the sesame seeds and spring onion greens and the rest of the soy mixture with it. Cook for a couple of minutes, just to warm through. You probably won't need to season this with salt as the soy sauce is very salty, but add a little black pepper, if you like.

Divide the stir-fry into four bowls and sprinkle over the remaining sesame seeds and spring onion greens. Serve with rice.

Serves 4
–
Prep 10 mins
–
Cook 15 mins

Meat

SLOW-COOKED BEEF & FENNEL CASSEROLE WITH DUMPLINGS

For cheap cuts of meat, such as the braising cuts used here, frozen choices are great – as not only are they economical, but freezing is said to tenderize meat. Although, unfortunately, you're unlikely to find fennel in the freezer aisle, fresh bulbs do freeze relatively well, and while they may not be fit for a fresh, crisp salad, on defrosting they will certainly be fine for a comforting stew such as this one.

2 tbsp olive oil
500g (1lb 2oz) frozen casserole, stewing or braising beef, defrosted
1 onion, sliced (or 200g/7oz frozen diced onion)
2 celery sticks, sliced
1 tbsp chopped frozen garlic (or 2 fresh cloves, finely chopped)
2 large fennel bulbs, cut into wedges (chop any attached fronds and set aside)
200g (7oz) frozen sliced carrots (or 2 fresh carrots, peeled and sliced)
2 tsp Dijon mustard
300ml (10½fl oz/1¼ cups) cider
300ml (10½fl oz/1¼ cups) hot rich beef stock
pared orange zest from ½ small orange (use a potato peeler to pare wide strips)
2 bay leaves
sea salt and ground black pepper

For the dumplings
175g (6oz/1⅓ cups) self-raising flour, plus extra for your hands
1 tsp fennel seeds, roughly ground in a pestle and mortar
80g (2¾oz/5½ tbsp) butter, diced
80ml (2½fl oz/5½ tbsp) milk

Preheat the oven to 160°C/315°F/gas mark 2–3.

Heat 1 tbsp of the olive oil in a large casserole dish and fry half of the beef over a high heat until browned. Scoop the meat out with a slotted spoon and transfer to a bowl, then repeat, adding 1 more tbsp of oil and the remaining beef. Scoop the meat out again, leaving all the oil in the pan.

Turn the heat down to medium–low and add the onion and celery to the pan. Sauté gently for 5 minutes or so until the onion has softened. Add the garlic and fennel and cook for a further 5 minutes. Add the carrots, then add the mustard, cider and the hot stock and bring the liquid to the boil. Add the pared orange zest and the bay leaves. Pop on a lid, transfer the pan to the preheated oven and cook for 1 hour.

Remove the pan from the oven and give everything a good stir, then return the pan to the oven for another 30 minutes.

Meanwhile, make the dumplings. Put the flour, ground fennel seeds and a good pinch of salt and pepper in a bowl and add the butter. Rub in using the tips of your fingers until you have a crumbly mixture. Add the milk to the bowl and use a dinner knife to mix everything until it starts to come together into a dough. Divide into 12 portions and, with floured hands, roll each one into a rough ball.

Remove the casserole from the oven and taste and season with salt and pepper. Add the dumplings to the top of the mixture. Cover again and return the pan to the oven for 20 minutes, then remove the pan lid and cook for 10–15 minutes longer, or until the dumplings are risen and fluffy and the tops are beginning to brown.

Serve the casserole at the table in the pan, sprinkling the top with the reserved chopped fennel fronds.

Will it re-freeze?
Yes, this is a good one for batch cooking and freezing. Freeze in foil trays and pop straight in an oven preheated to 180°C/350°F/gas mark 4 for about 30 minutes. Cover the top of the tray with foil if the dumplings are getting too brown.

Serves 4
–
Prep 30 mins
–
Cook 2½ hours

LEBANESE LAMB FLATBREADS

These are a quick and delicious way to utilize a pack of frozen lamb mince. Frozen mince is often not super lean, which is perfect for this as no extra liquid is added to the mix, so a little natural fat keeps the topping from drying out. I like to use Greek-style flatbreads (and generally have a pack in the freezer for emergencies), but you could use pita breads too, if that's what you happen to have to hand.

1 tbsp olive oil
150g (5½oz) frozen diced onion (or 1 small onion, finely diced)
1 tbsp Lebanese seven-spice powder
1 tbsp chopped frozen garlic (or 2 fresh cloves, finely chopped)
350g (12oz) frozen minced (ground) lamb (15–20% fat), defrosted
2 tbsp tomato purée (paste)
50g (1¾oz) dried cherries
sea salt

To serve
4 flatbreads (fresh or frozen)
4–8 tbsp thick Greek yogurt
a few mint leaves, roughly chopped

Preheat the oven to 160°C/315°F/gas mark 2–3.

Heat the oil in a large frying or sauté pan and add the onion and seven-spice. Cook gently over a medium–low heat for about 8 minutes, or until the onion is soft and translucent. Add the garlic and cook for another minute or so.

Turn the heat up to medium–high and add the lamb. Fry for a few minutes until it is all brown and cooked, and starting to turn golden in places. Stir in the tomato purée and the cherries and cook for another couple of minutes, then season to taste with salt.

Once the lamb is cooked, heat the flatbreads. If fresh, place them in the oven for a couple of minutes to warm. You can also cook them straight from frozen by increasing the cooking time to 8–10 minutes.

Lay the flatbreads out on plates and spread each one with 1–2 tbsp Greek yogurt. Divide the lamb mixture between the breads and finish with a sprinkling of mint leaves. Serve while the lamb and bread are still warm.

Freezer adaptation:
You could use minced beef for this, too, if you don't happen to have lamb, although lamb is hard to beat here.

Will it re-freeze?
The lamb mixture freezes really well, so freeze it in individual portions and you can just defrost one and reheat it in the microwave to assemble a fresh flatbread in no time.

Serves 4
–
Prep 5 mins
–
Cook 20 mins

Meat

LITTLE VEGGIE-LOADED SHEPHERD'S PIES

This is a great recipe for perking up freezer mince, using up freezer veg, and also making sure you pack your dinner with plenty of healthy veggies – especially if you serve a portion of green freezer veg on the side. You can also combine standard mash with sweet potato mash, as I have here, which you can now buy frozen, to up your vitamin intake even more.

2 tbsp olive oil
200g (7oz) frozen chopped onion
(or 1 onion, diced)
2 celery sticks, sliced
200g (7oz) frozen sliced carrots
(or 2 carrots, peeled and sliced)
½ tbsp frozen chopped garlic
(or 1 fresh clove, finely chopped)
400g (14oz) frozen minced (ground) lamb
250g (9oz) frozen sliced mushrooms
2 bushy sprigs frozen (or fresh) rosemary
2 tbsp tomato purée (paste)
1 tsp dried mint
a good pinch of ground allspice
1 lamb jelly stock pot or cube
150g (5½oz) frozen peas
400g (14oz) chunks of frozen mashed potato or sweet potato
(or a combination of both)
50g (1¾oz) Cheddar cheese, grated
sea salt and ground black pepper

Will it re-freeze?

I purposely assemble these in individual enamel pie dishes so that they can be thrown in the oven straight from the freezer. You can use foil trays for this too. Bake at 180°C/350°F/gas mark 4 for 30–40 minutes, covering the top with a piece of foil if it looks as if it's browning too quickly.

Heat the oil in a large saucepan and add the onion. Cook over a low–medium heat for a few minutes until softening. Add the celery, carrots and garlic and cook for 5 more minutes, then add the lamb and mushrooms. Cook for a couple of minutes until the lamb and mushrooms are defrosted, then add the rosemary, tomato purée, mint and allspice. Dissolve the stock pot in 300ml (10½fl oz/1¼ cups) boiling water and add this too. Pop a lid on the pan and cook for 15 minutes, stirring occasionally. Meanwhile, preheat the oven to 180°C/350°F/gas mark 4.

Take the lid off the pan and continue cooking until the liquid is reduced and you have a thick sauce – about 15 minutes longer. Turn off the heat, season to taste with salt and pepper and stir in the frozen peas. Set aside while you prepare the topping.

Place the cubes of frozen mash in a heatproof bowl, cover and microwave as per the packet instructions – usually about 3 minutes. Beat until smooth.

Divide the filling between individual pie dishes, then spoon the mash over the top of the filling. Sprinkle the tops of the pies with grated cheese and pop them in the oven. Bake for about 25 minutes, or until the filling is reheated, the cheese is melted and the tops are golden. (Note, if the filling has cooled to room temperature, the pies may take longer to heat through again.) Serve immediately with green freezer veggies or a salad.

Serves 4
–
Prep 15 mins
–
Cook 1 hour

MEATBALLS WITH PEPERONATA, CHEESY POLENTA & CRISPY FRIED CAPERS

You can use all pork for these meatballs, as here, or if you're using up bits and bobs, feel free to try a mixture of pork and beef mince.

For the meatballs
3 tbsp olive oil
1 small red onion, finely diced
1 garlic clove, crushed
1 tsp dried thyme
500g (1lb 2oz) frozen minced
   (ground) pork
3–6 tbsp frozen breadcrumbs
sea salt and ground black pepper

For the peperonata
2 tbsp olive oil
1 large red onion, sliced
1½ tbsp frozen chopped garlic (or
   3 fresh cloves, finely chopped)
500g (1lb 2oz) frozen sliced peppers
1 × 400g (14oz) can chopped tomatoes
2 tsp red wine vinegar
1 tsp sugar

For the capers
a drizzle of olive oil
4 tbsp baby capers or capers

For the polenta
200g (7oz) quick cook polenta
   (cornmeal)
80g (3oz) finely grated Parmesan

Will it re-freeze?

Yes, the meatballs and sauce are good recipes for batch freezing. Defrost and reheat in the microwave.

```
Serves 4
–
Prep 30 mins
–
Cook 1 hour
```

For the meatballs, heat 1 tbsp of the oil in a large sauté pan and add the onion. Fry gently for 5 minutes until soft, then add the garlic and thyme and cook for 2 minutes. Leave to cool.

Put the pork into a large bowl and add the cooled onion mix. Add 3 tbsp of the breadcrumbs and mix in well (it's easiest to get your hands in the mix to do this). The amount of crumbs required depends on how much water is in the meat, so if the mixture is not clumping together and feels wet, add a little more. Season well with salt and pepper. Roll the mixture into balls a little larger than a walnut (you should get about 16).

Heat the remaining 2 tbsp of oil in the sauté pan and fry half of the meatballs, turning regularly, until they are browned all over. Remove them from the pan with tongs or a slotted spoon and set aside, then fry the remaining meatballs and, once browned, set those aside too. Wipe out the pan.

For the peperonata, add the oil to the pan and fry the red onion for 8 minutes or so until well softened. Add the garlic and fry for a couple more minutes, then add the peppers and tomatoes. Add a splash of water to the can, swirl it around and tip that in too. Increase the heat to high and bring the liquid to a boil, then reduce the heat to a simmer and cook the sauce for 30 minutes, uncovered, until it has reduced down and thickened. Meanwhile, bring 900ml (31fl oz/4 cups) water to the boil in a saucepan.

Once the 30 minutes are up, add the vinegar and sugar to the sauce and season well with salt and pepper. Return the meatballs to the pan and tuck them into the sauce, then put a lid on the pan and cook for another 10 minutes, until the meatballs are cooked through.

For the capers, add a drizzle of oil to a frying pan over a high heat and add the capers. Fry for about 5 minutes until crisp.

Add the polenta to the boiling water in the pan, pouring it in a slow stream while beating with a spoon. Add the Parmesan and keep beating over the heat for about 2 minutes, until the polenta is thickened and no longer gritty. Season well.

To serve, divide the polenta between four serving plates and top with the meatballs and sauce. Sprinkle with the capers and a little more Parmesan, and chopped parsley, if you like.

SMOKY SAUSAGE, SWEET POTATO & BUTTER BEAN STEW

This is satisfying, warming post-winter-walk fare. Cook it the day before and just reheat when you return for instant comfort in a bowl. Serve with crusty bread or, to make it more of a meal, with gnocchi – if you happen to have some in the freezer – or soft polenta. It makes a big batch purposely as it freezes brilliantly, ready for a quick flash in the microwave after a long day at work.

2 tbsp olive oil
12 frozen pork sausages, defrosted
1 onion, sliced (or 200g/7oz frozen diced onion)
3 celery stalks, sliced
1½ tbsp chopped frozen garlic (or 3 fresh cloves, finely chopped)
2 × 400g (14oz) cans chopped tomatoes
1 tbsp sweet smoked paprika
1 tsp Worcestershire sauce
2 tsp Dijon mustard
¼ tsp ground cinnamon
a largish sprig of rosemary (frozen or fresh)
1 chicken jelly stock pot
600g (1lb 5oz) frozen sweet potato
2 × 400g (14oz) cans butter (lima) beans, drained and rinsed
sea salt and ground black pepper
crusty bread, to serve

Heat the oil in a large saucepan or casserole dish over a high heat and brown the sausages on all sides – you will probably need to do this in batches. Once browned, remove them from the pan with tongs, leaving the oil in the pan, and lower the heat to low–medium.

Add the onion and celery to the pan and cook for 8 minutes or so until soft. Add the garlic and cook for another couple of minutes, then add the tomatoes and stir. Now add the seasonings – the paprika, Worcestershire sauce, mustard, cinnamon, rosemary and stock pot – along with 300ml (10½fl oz/1¼ cups) water. Add the frozen sweet potato and stir everything together. Increase the heat and bring everything almost to boiling, then reduce to low–medium, cover the pan with a lid and leave to simmer for 20 minutes, stirring occasionally.

Once the 20 minutes are up, remove the lid, add the butter beans and return the sausages to the pan. Cook, uncovered, for another 20 minutes or so to cook the sausages through and reduce and thicken the sauce, giving it a stir more frequently now. Season to taste with salt and pepper.

Serve the stew with hunks of fresh crusty bread.

Freezer adaptation:
If you don't have enough sweet potato, you can make up the weight with frozen carrot or butternut squash instead.

Will it re-freeze?
Yes, this is a good one for batch cooking. Simply defrost and reheat gently in the microwave.

Serves 6
–
Prep 10 mins
–
Cook 1 hour

FREEZER FEAST: CHICKEN CASSOULET

This French countryside-inspired feast uses up a host of freezer staples – from meats to veg, herbs and breadcrumbs – along with a few basics from the pantry. There's actually no breadcrumbs on top in the authentic version, but there is a reason people are so wedded to their addition, so they are present if not entirely correct here.

2 tbsp olive oil
4–6 frozen pork sausages, defrosted
4 frozen chicken leg quarters, defrosted (or you could use duck legs, if you happen to have those frozen)
160g (5¾oz) smoked bacon lardons, defrosted if frozen
1 large onion, finely sliced (or 250g/9oz frozen diced onion)
1 tsp fennel seeds
200g (7oz) frozen sliced carrots (or 2 fresh carrots, peeled and sliced)
2 celery sticks, sliced
2 tbsp chopped frozen garlic (or 4 fresh cloves, finely chopped)
leaves from 3 sprigs thyme (frozen or fresh)
2 tbsp tomato purée (paste)
400ml (14fl oz) hot chicken stock
2 × 400g (14oz) cans cannellini beans, drained
2 large tomatoes, deseeded and diced
a grating of whole nutmeg or a pinch of ground
1 tbsp butter
60g (2oz) fresh breadcrumbs
sea salt and ground black pepper

Preheat the oven to 180°C/350°F/gas mark 4.

Heat the oil in a large, shallow casserole dish over a high heat. Brown the sausages for a few minutes, turning regularly until browned all over. Remove them from the pan and add the chicken legs. Do the same, browning for a few minutes all over, then remove them from the pan, too. Finally, add the lardons to the pan and cook until turning golden.

Turn the heat down to medium–low and add the sliced onion, fennel seeds and a pinch of salt. Sauté for a few minutes until the onion is softening, then add the carrot, celery, garlic and thyme to the pan. Sauté for a few more minutes until all the veg is starting to soften.

Stir the tomato purée into the hot stock, then pour the stock over the veg. Return the sausages and chicken legs to the pan, keeping the skin of the chicken above the liquid in the pan, if you can. Cover the whole pan with a lid or a piece of foil and place in the oven for 1 hour.

After an hour, remove the chicken from the top and stir in the beans and fresh tomatoes. Season well with salt and pepper and stir in the nutmeg, then replace the chicken on top. Re-cover and return to the oven for another 30 minutes.

In the meantime, melt the butter in a frying pan, then stir in the fresh crumbs until they are all coated in the butter.

Once that 30 minutes are up, sprinkle the breadcrumbs all over the top of the cassoulet. Return the pan to the oven, this time without the lid. Cook for a final 15 minutes, or until the crumbs are crispy and golden. Serve with a salad or green freezer veg and a glass of white wine.

Will it re-freeze?

Yes! Decant any leftovers into a baking dish or foil tray, trying to keep the chicken and crumbs on top. Cover with the tray lid or a piece of foil, label and freeze. When you are ready to eat it, let it thaw first, then return it to the oven at 180°C/350°F/gas mark 4 for about 30 minutes.

Serves 4
–
Prep 20 mins
–
Cook 2 hours

MOROCCAN CHICKEN & CAULIFLOWER TRAYBAKE

The joy of this recipe is that although it may have a long-ish ingredients list, if you have a well-stocked freezer and store cupboard, you are likely to have most of them already. After a bit of marinating, you can also just chuck it all in the oven knowing it will come out as a complete dinner, with no more work required. This is quite mild, but if you'd like it a bit hotter, add more harissa for an extra spicy kick.

4 tbsp olive oil
1 garlic clove, crushed (you can also use frozen chopped garlic here, but may have to crush it a bit more)
1½ tsp ground coriander
1 tsp ground turmeric
2 tsp ground cumin
1 lemon
4 frozen chicken legs, defrosted
1 tbsp harissa
1 large onion, cut into slim wedges
500g (1lb 2oz) frozen cauliflower florets
2 cinnamon sticks
50g (1¾oz) flaked almonds (or blanched hazelnuts)
2 × 400g (14oz) cans chickpeas, drained and rinsed
75g (2½oz) dried apricots, halved if small, quartered if larger
a handful of parsley, roughly chopped (or a sprinkling of frozen chopped parsley)
sea salt and ground black pepper
green salad, to serve

Mix the oil with the garlic, coriander, turmeric, cumin and a good pinch of salt. Zest half of the lemon. Drizzle half of the spiced oil over the chicken legs and sprinkle with the lemon zest. Rub it all over the chicken legs, cover and leave in the fridge to marinate for a couple of hours. (You can marinate these while still frozen and leave to thaw in the fridge for a day so they really absorb the flavours as they thaw out.)

Preheat the oven to 190°C/375°F/gas mark 5.

Add the harissa to the remaining half of the spiced oil and stir in well.

Place the onion wedges in a roasting pan. Slice the partially zested lemon into wedges and scatter among the onion in the pan, then add the frozen cauliflower florets and the cinnamon sticks. Drizzle the spiced harissa oil over everything in the pan and toss to coat – the easiest way to do this is to get your hands in there. Arrange the marinated chicken pieces over the top of the veg and place in the oven for 30 minutes.

Meanwhile, toast the flaked almonds in a frying pan (or put on a baking tray in the oven for a few minutes) until golden and smelling toasty. Remove from the pan and set aside.

After the chicken has had 30 minutes, remove the pan from the oven and remove the chicken legs to a plate with tongs. Add the chickpeas and dried apricots to the pan and give everything a good stir. Return the chicken legs to the top and return to the oven for 20–25 minutes, or until the chicken is golden and cooked through, the veg is tender and the chickpeas are warmed. Sprinkle with the toasted almonds, parsley and a little more seasoning, and serve with a green salad.

Will it re-freeze?

The cauliflower will, admittedly, be a bit mushy by the time it's refrozen and defrosted. But everything else freezes well and will all be delicious on thawing and reheating gently – just pop it in the microwave.

Serves 4
–
Prep 10 mins
–
Cook 55 mins

SMOKY & SPICY BUTTERMILK DRUMMERS

This recipe not only uses economical cuts of chicken that you can find in pretty much any freezer aisle, but also one of my most-used homemade freezer staples – fresh breadcrumbs. If you haven't got any buttermilk, you can always make a substitute with milk and lemon juice (see ingredients list), which will provide a sticky surface for the flavoursome crumbs to adhere to.

1kg (2lb 4oz) chicken drumsticks (about 8–10), thawed
300ml (10½fl oz/1¼ cups) buttermilk (or combine the same amount of whole milk and 1 tbsp lemon juice and leave for 10 minutes for a buttermilk substitute)
oil or butter, for greasing
120g (4¼oz) frozen or fresh breadcrumbs
barbecue sauce, mayo, aioli, ketchup or dip of your choice, to serve

For the spice mix
2 tbsp sweet smoked paprika
2 tsp garlic granules
1 tbsp dried thyme
2 tsp dried ancho chilli flakes
2 tbsp smoked sea salt flakes

Freezer adaptation:
You can easily use chicken thighs or whole leg pieces if you don't have drumsticks.

Will it re-freeze?
Yes, although the crumbs may not be as crispy nor the chicken as juicy by the time they are defrosted and reheated – these are best eaten fresh.

Tip the drumsticks into a large bowl and pour over the buttermilk. Stir so that the chicken is all evenly coated, then cover the bowl with clingfilm (plastic wrap) and pop it in the fridge to marinate for a few hours – the longer the better, and you can do this overnight if you wish.

When you are ready to cook, preheat the oven to 200°C/400°F/gas mark 6 and lightly grease a large baking tray. Bring the chicken out of the fridge to come up to room temperature for 30 minutes or so while the oven heats.

Meanwhile, combine all of the ingredients for the spice mix in a small bowl.

Tip the breadcrumbs into a large shallow dish, such as a large plate or baking dish. Add the spice mix and stir together well.

Pick a drumstick out of the buttermilk, holding it by the knobbly end, and shake off any excess buttermilk over the bowl. Transfer it to the dish with the crumbs and roll it around in the mixture until it is coated, then place on the prepared baking sheet. Repeat to coat all of the drumsticks.

Put the tray in the oven and cook the chicken for 45 minutes, until golden on the outside and tender throughout. Enjoy fresh from the oven with dips of your choice.

Serves 4
–
Prep 5 mins
–
Cook 45 mins

Meat

CHICKEN SATAY SKEWERS WITH COOL MANGO SALSA

These are delicious cooked over coals on a barbecue, but even in a griddle pan on the hob you can achieve a lovely, charred caramelization. Balance all that with a tangy mango salsa made from frozen mango and chilli and you have a perfect summery sharing dish.

500g (1lb 2oz) frozen chicken breast, defrosted
2 tbsp smooth peanut butter
2 tbsp dark soy sauce
1 tbsp clear runny honey
finely grated zest and squeezed juice from ½ lime
½ tbsp frozen chopped garlic (or 1 fresh clove, finely chopped)
1 tbsp frozen (or fresh) chopped ginger
½ tbsp frozen (or fresh) chopped red chilli
olive oil, for drizzling

For the spice mix
1 tsp ground cumin
1 tsp ground coriander
½ tsp ground turmeric
½ tsp chilli powder (mild or hot as wished)
1 tsp sea salt flakes

For the mango salsa
125g (4½oz) frozen mango chunks
½ small red onion, finely diced
½ tbsp frozen chopped red chilli
zest and juice from ½ lime
a few fresh coriander (cilantro) leaves, chopped (or use chopped frozen)

Once the chicken is thawed enough to cut safely, slice it lengthways into long strips. Put them in a large bowl.

Combine all the ingredients for the spice mix and toss the chicken in the spices until they are well covered.

Combine the peanut butter, soy sauce, honey, lime zest and juice, garlic, ginger, chilli and a good pinch of salt in a bowl and stir until smooth. Pour this over the chicken, cover and leave in the fridge for a couple of hours to marinate.

Meanwhile, make the salsa. Wait until the mango is defrosted enough to cut (it can still be a little frozen) and dice it into smaller cubes. Pop it in a bowl and add all the remaining ingredients, along with a pinch of salt. Chill in the fridge while you prepare the skewers.

Once the chicken is well flavoured, you're ready to assemble. Thread the chicken strips onto skewers, looping the strips back and forward as you fold. Don't push the folds up too close to each other or they won't cook very evenly. Thread about 2–3 long strips onto each skewer – you should be able to make 8 or so skewers. Leave them to come up to room temperature before you cook.

Heat a griddle pan with a drizzle of oil, or light a barbecue and drizzle a little oil directly over the skewers. Place the skewers over the heat and cook for about 7–8 minutes, turning occasionally, or until well browned all over (charred in places) and cooked through. Serve the skewers with the mango salsa.

Will it re-freeze?
You could re-freeze the skewers once cooked. Or, a better option is to make them from fresh chicken, marinating and assembling them before freezing. On the day of a big family get-together, you know that this bit of prep is already done; just let them defrost, drizzle with oil and pop them on the barbecue to char to perfection.

Serves 4
–
Prep 15 mins
–
Cook 8 mins

CHICKEN, CHORIZO & MED VEG ORZO BAKE

At most supermarkets now, you can find bags of delicious mixed Mediterranean vegetables in the freezer section, which are often pre-griddled for a flavour boost. Freezer products like these are what makes it so easy to make healthy, homemade, fuss-free meals so much more accessible for the time poor. Just think how much time you save not having to chop and griddle all the veg first.

150g (5½oz) chorizo, sliced
a drizzle of olive oil (optional)
4 small frozen chicken breasts, defrosted
500g (1lb 2oz) frozen grilled Mediterranean vegetables
1 tbsp frozen chopped garlic (or 2 fresh cloves, finely chopped)
1 × 400g (14oz) can chopped tomatoes
200g (7oz) orzo pasta
a few black olives (optional)
400ml (14fl oz/1¾ cups) hot chicken stock
a handful of basil leaves, shredded, plus extra leaves to serve
20g (⅔oz) Parmesan cheese, grated
sea salt and ground black pepper
salad leaves, to serve (optional)

Preheat the oven to 180°C/350°F/gas mark 4.

Heat a large non-stick frying pan over a medium–high heat and add the chorizo. Cook until browned, then remove with a slotted spoon, leaving the oil in the pan. If the chorizo hasn't let out much oil, add a drizzle to the pan to stop the chicken sticking. Add the chicken breasts to the pan and cook for a few minutes on each side until they have plenty of colour all over (they don't need to be cooked through yet) and remove from the pan with a slotted spoon.

Add the veg to the pan along with the garlic and cook for a couple of minutes until heated through and browning, then return the chicken and chorizo to the pan, along with the tomatoes. Let them heat through for a couple of minutes.

Tip the chicken and vegetable mix into a large baking dish and add the orzo, olives (if using) and hot stock. Sprinkle over the chopped basil, season with salt and pepper and mix until everything is well combined. Cover with foil and transfer the dish to the oven. Bake for 25 minutes.

Once the 25 minutes is up, the orzo should be cooked and the sauce thickened. Sprinkle the top of the bake with the Parmesan and return to the oven for a final 5 minutes, until the cheese is melted. Sprinkle with a few more basil leaves and serve with some green leaves on the side, if you like.

Freezer adaptation:
The bags of mixed frozen Mediterranean veg are generally quite heavy on the peppers, so if you just have a bag of plain sliced frozen peppers, these will work too.

Will it re-freeze?
Yes, and this works well for a quick freezer dinner with all your required veg included – although a bag of fresh salad leaves wouldn't go amiss. Simply allow to defrost naturally, then reheat in the microwave or back in the oven.

Serves 4
–
Prep 15 mins
–
Cook 40 mins

FISH

Fish always feels like an intuitive product to buy frozen, as it's so often frozen at sea upon catch, keeping it wonderfully fresh. For meals that use fewer ingredients, other than what you find in the freezer, try the Miso Salmon Broth or the Prawny Pot Stickers. Choices to please the whole family include a classic Fish Pie and Kedgeree, and for feeding a crowd, try a platter of Tempura, assemble-yourself Blackened Tuna Tacos, or a Paella freezer feast (pictured here).

THE ULTIMATE FISH FINGER SARNIE P

Fish fingers are a freezer staple, but sometimes they need a little dressing up, so try this, the best of butties. Usually I'm a strong advocate for sourdough, but not for this recipe. Fish fingers require something a little fluffier, preferably baked that day and sliced at home into doorstop-style hunks. Team with fancy salted butter – preferably the stuff that's golden in hue and has crystals of salt in it.

12 chunky fish fingers
8 thick slices very fresh white crusty
    bread
good, salted butter, for spreading
4 small handfuls of rocket (arugula)
lemon wedges, for squeezing

For the tartare sauce
4 heaped tbsp mayonnaise (the nice
    French sort, if you fancy a treat)
3 tbsp finely diced pickled gherkins
1 heaped tbsp drained capers, roughly
    chopped
2 tsp lemon juice
1 tbsp finely chopped tarragon
½ tsp finely grated lemon zest
sea salt and ground black pepper

Begin by making the tartare sauce, so it's good to go when your fish fingers are fresh out the oven. Combine all the measured ingredients in a small bowl and season to taste with salt and pepper.

Cook the fish fingers according to the packet instructions. (I like to oven cook mine as there's less chance of them catching on top.)

While the fish fingers cook, set up your sarnie production line! Butter all the bread and lay out four slices. Divide the tartare sauce between them and spread out. Sprinkle a small handful of rocket over each slice.

Once the fish fingers are cooked, divide them between the slices and sandwich together with the remaining bread. Eat immediately with lemon wedges for squeezing over the fish.

Freezer adaptation:
This also works well with vegetarian sausages, although they do differ a lot in flavour, so some experimentation may be required to find ones that go with the other trimmings.

Will it re-freeze?
No, but any leftover sauce will keep in a sealed container in the fridge for a few days.

Serves 4
–
Prep 10 mins
–
Cook 20 mins

PRAWNY POT STICKERS P

These irresistible dumplings can be filled almost entirely from ingredients that you can buy in the freezer aisle, plus a few pantry seasonings. I like to use spring onions too, which I generally always have in the fridge, but these aren't essential. Dumpling wrappers can be found in most international supermarkets, either frozen or in the chilled food aisle.

cornflour (cornstarch), for dusting
14–16 gyoza dumpling wrappers, defrosted if frozen
2 tbsp vegetable oil, for frying

For the gyoza filling
200g (7oz) frozen small cooked prawns (shrimp), defrosted
3 spring onions (scallions), finely chopped (optional)
60g (2oz) frozen edamame beans, defrosted
1 tsp frozen chopped garlic (or 1 small fresh clove, finely chopped)
2 tsp frozen (or fresh) chopped ginger
½ tsp frozen (or fresh) chopped chilli
1½ tbsp oyster sauce
½ tbsp sesame oil
a pinch of salt

For the dipping sauce
3 tbsp soy sauce
1 tbsp rice vinegar
2 tsp sesame oil
1 tbsp toasted sesame seeds
½ tbsp frozen chopped chilli

Will it re-freeze?

Not really; these are best eaten fresh out the pan.

Combine all the ingredients for the gyoza filling, reserving a few sliced spring onion greens to sprinkle over at the end (if using).

Dust a small plate lightly with cornflour, ready to receive the dumplings.

Place a dumpling wrapper on a work surface and, using a finger, dampen all around the edge with a little water. Spoon about 1 tbsp of the filling mix into the centre of the dumpling wrapper and fold up the bare edge from each side to meet in the middle above the filling. Crimp the edges across the top to seal, then set on the floured plate. Repeat to fill the remaining dumpling wrappers.

Heat 1 tbsp of the vegetable oil in a large non-stick frying or sauté pan (with an accompanying lid). Once hot, add half of the pot stickers and fry for 2–3 minutes until the bottoms are golden.

Pour 3 tbsp water into the pan and quickly pop the lid on. Turn the heat down to low–medium and steam the dumplings for about 3 minutes, until cooked through. Transfer them to a plate lined with kitchen paper, then repeat to cook the remaining half of the dumplings.

While the dumplings are steaming, combine all the ingredients for the dipping sauce.

Once all the dumplings are cooked, sprinkle them with the reserved spring onion greens, if using, and serve with the dipping sauce.

Serves 4
–
Prep 20 mins
–
Cook 15 mins

SEABASS CEVICHE WITH GRAPEFRUIT, CUCUMBER & MINT SALAD P

Freezer food doesn't always have to be about batch cooking economy; sometimes you want something a little more fancy. Look out for frozen bags of seabass fillets, which are great for this, and also those that are marked 'quick frozen'. Freshness is paramount as the fish will be 'cooked' only in the acid from the citrus fruits. This will serve two people as a meal, or makes a nice starter for four.

For the ceviche
2 frozen seabass fillets, defrosted
3 spring onions (scallions), very finely sliced
1–2 tsp chopped frozen (or fresh) red chilli (depending on how hot you want it)
1 tsp flaked sea salt
1 tsp finely grated pink grapefruit zest
freshly squeezed juice of ½ pink grapefruit
freshly squeezed juice of 1 lime

For the salad
1 cucumber
2 tbsp grapefruit juice
1 tsp finely grated pink grapefruit zest
1 tbsp olive oil
sea salt and ground black pepper
mint leaves, to serve

Remove the skin from the fish and slice the flesh into rough diamond shapes. Put it in a bowl with the remaining ceviche ingredients and stir together. Cover and place in the fridge for 2–3 hours to 'cook'.

To make the salad, pare the skin and flesh from the cucumber in thin strips using a vegetable peeler. Discard (or nibble on) the really seedy bit in the middle. Put the cucumber ribbons into a serving bowl.

Combine the grapefruit juice and zest and the olive oil in a small jug and season well with salt and pepper.

Strain the ceviche to get rid of the fishy water and sprinkle the solids over the salad. Re-dress with the freshly made dressing and finish with a sprinkle of fresh, torn mint leaves.

Freezer adaptation:
You could also add some blanched (and cooled) frozen peas or edamame beans to the salad to make it a little more substantial.

Will it re-freeze?
Because the fish isn't technically cooked, you shouldn't re-freeze this.

Serves 2–4
–
Prep 15 mins
–
'Cook' 3 hours

SEAFOOD TEMPURA P

A simple but moreish platter of tempura can be magicked up from the freezer if you always keep a stock of frozen fish. Supermarkets usually do a pretty wide range – from basic white fish that can be cut into strips, to all sorts of squid, prawns, whitebait and seafood mixes. Use as many or as few types of different seafoods that you have available – it will all taste great.

sunflower or vegetable oil, for frying
about 600g (1lb 5oz) frozen raw
    seafood (white fish, squid rings,
    large shelled prawns/shrimp,
    whitebait, baby octopus,
    etc.), defrosted
50g (1¾oz/heaped ⅓ cup) plain
    (all-purpose) flour
50g (1¾oz/½ cup) cornflour
    (cornstarch)
½ tsp fine salt
150ml (5fl oz/scant ⅔ cup) very cold
    sparkling water

To serve
sea salt flakes
aioli
lemon wedges

First, put your oil on to heat. A deep fat fryer is best for this, but you can also fry the tempura in a deep saucepan.

Now prepare your fish. Cut any large fillets of fish into strips and pat everything dry with kitchen paper.

Sift the flours and salt into a bowl. Add the ice-cold water and stir everything together until just combined. Don't whisk too much or the gluten in the flour will develop and the batter will become heavy.

To test if the oil is hot enough, dip a small piece of your seafood into the batter and pop it in the saucepan. If it sizzles and bubbles gently when added to the oil, you're good to go.

Cook the seafood in batches – being careful not to over-crowd the pan so that it crisps up and doesn't go soggy – for a few minutes until light golden. The cooking time will vary depending on the seafood, but take a piece out of the oil and test that it is cooked through. Remove from the oil with a slotted spoon and drain on kitchen paper before cooking the next batch.

Pile the seafood onto a platter and sprinkle with sea salt. Serve with a pot of aioli for dipping and wedges of lemon to squeeze over.

Will it re-freeze?

If you have leftovers, these could be frozen to save them for another day. Allow to defrost, then reheat gently on a baking tray in the oven. The time will depend on what the item is and how big, but no more than 10 minutes should be fine.

Serves 4
–
Prep 5 mins
–
Cook 20 mins

KEDGEREE P

Combine frozen fish and veg with a few pantry basics in this Anglo-Indian classic which never seems to get tired. Everyone should have a kedgeree recipe in their pocket as it's such a great one-pot dish – and if it uses stuff you happen to have in your freezer (fish, peas, onion, etc.), all the better.

400ml (14fl oz/1¾ cups) whole milk
500g (1lb 2oz) frozen smoked haddock, defrosted
30g (2 tbsp) butter
1 tbsp vegetable oil
250g (9oz) frozen diced onion
    (or 1 large onion, finely diced)
1 tbsp medium curry powder
1 tsp ground turmeric
250g (9oz) basmati rice
200g (7oz) frozen peas
4 medium eggs
a bunch of parsley, leaves chopped,
    plus a few sprigs to serve
sea salt and ground black pepper
nigella seeds, for sprinkling
lemon wedges, for squeezing over

Freezer adaptation:

If you don't have frozen peas (as if), you could use frozen green beans or frozen edamame at a stretch. Anything green will give this rich dish a lovely fresh boost.

Will it re-freeze?

Yes, just try not to mush the rice up too much on thawing. I recommend defrosting naturally, then reheating gently in the microwave.

Put the milk in a pan, add 200ml (7fl oz/scant 1 cup) water and bring to a simmer. Add the frozen haddock pieces and make sure they are submerged in the liquid. Simmer for 6–7 minutes until just cooked through and the fish is starting to flake.

Meanwhile, melt the butter with the oil in a sauté pan and add the onion and a good pinch of salt. Fry gently over a low–medium heat for 7–8 minutes until well softened. Add the spices and cook for a couple more minutes until everything is smelling aromatic. Add the rice and stir around in the fragrant oil for a minute or so.

Once the fish is cooked, scoop it out of the cooking liquid and set aside on a plate, covered with foil to keep it warm. Measure 350ml (12fl oz/1½ cups) of the cooking liquid and add it to the rice pan, along with another 300ml (10½fl oz/1¼ cups) water. Turn up the heat and bring the milk to a simmer. Put a lid on the pan and cook for 6 minutes without lifting the lid. Meanwhile, bring a pan of water to the boil for the eggs.

Remove the lid and stir in the peas. Cover and cook for a further 5 minutes. Then turn off the heat and leave it to rest with the lid on for another 8 minutes.

Meanwhile, flake the haddock into large pieces. Add the eggs to the boiling water and cook for 7 minutes, until hard boiled but the yolk is still quite soft and golden.

Remove the lid from the pan and fluff up the rice. Stir in the haddock, being careful not to break it up too much, and the chopped parsley. Season with salt and pepper – you probably won't need much more salt as the smoked fish is quite salty.

Divide the kedgeree between four serving bowls and top each bowl with a halved boiled egg. Sprinkle over a few nigella seeds and finish with a few sprigs of parsley. Serve with lemon wedges for squeezing over.

Serves 4
–
Prep 15 mins
–
Cook 30 mins

BLACKENED CAJUN TUNA TACOS WITH FREEZER GUACAMOLE P

Fresh tuna steaks are a world away from the canned stuff, but they can be prohibitively expensive. Buying your steaks frozen is a much cheaper way to enjoy them. Just let them thaw out in their own time in the fridge. Avocados too can be pricey to buy fresh, but frozen avocado makes decent guacamole and is far more economical. Add some tacos and a few select salad items for an assemble-yourself feast.

4 frozen tuna steaks, defrosted
1 tbsp olive oil
1 tbsp Cajun seasoning

For the pickled red onions:
½ small red onion, very finely sliced
freshy squeezed juice of 1 lime

For the guacamole
200g (7oz) frozen avocado
  (halves or diced), defrosted
  (or use fresh avocado)
freshy squeezed juice of 1 lime
sea salt

To serve
8 soft corn tacos
soured cream (optional)
shredded iceberg lettuce
chopped fresh tomato
sliced fresh chillies (optional)
fresh coriander (cilantro) sprigs
  (optional)
lime wedges

Start by marinating the tuna. Pat the tuna dry with kitchen paper if defrosting has left them feeling a little slippery. Put them in a shallow dish and drizzle over the oil. Make sure they are coated, then sprinkle over the Cajun seasoning, ensuring you season both sides of the steaks. Cover, put the steaks back in the fridge and leave to marinate for a couple of hours.

To make the pickled onions, put the onions in a shallow bowl and pour over the lime juice. Stir well, then cover and leave to pickle for 30 minutes or so, stirring occasionally.

To make the guacamole, roughly chop the avocado if using halves, or just put the diced avocado into a bowl. Using a fork, potato masher or utensil of your choice, mash the avocado until you have a chunky paste. Add the lime juice and stir in, then taste and season with salt. Place a piece of clingfilm (plastic wrap) over the surface of the guacamole so the air can't get in and turn it brown, then chill in the fridge until needed.

Once the tuna is marinated, heat a non-stick frying pan over a very high heat. Cook the tuna steaks for about 1 minute on each side, until the spices are blackening on the outside but the fish is still pink in the middle. Remove them from the pan, then slice into thick strips.

To serve, lay out the sliced tuna along with the guacamole, pickled onions, tacos, soured cream and salad bits. Let your guests assemble their tacos how they wish and enjoy.

Freezer adaptation:

You don't need to use tuna for this. Any fish fillets (cod, salmon, etc.) you happen to have in the freezer would also work.

Will it re-freeze?

Not really. Best to prepare all this fresh.

Serves 4
–
Prep 30 mins
–
Cook 3 mins

MISO SALMON & FREEZER VEG NOODLE BROTH P

This broth is proof that you can prepare a fresh, healthy and reviving bowl of goodness with ingredients almost entirely from your freezer. This makes two generous portions and is ready in no time.

2 tbsp vegetable oil
1 tbsp frozen chopped garlic (or
    2 fresh cloves, finely chopped)
½ tbsp frozen (or fresh)
    chopped ginger
small bunch of spring onions
    (scallions) sliced and white
    and green parts separated
150g (5½oz) frozen sliced mushrooms
80g (2¾oz) dried soba or udon noodles
100g (3½oz) sliced frozen carrots
    (or 1 carrot, peeled and sliced)
700ml (24fl oz/3 cups) hot good-quality
    fish stock
120g (4¼oz) frozen edamame beans
100g (3½oz) frozen sweetcorn
2 tsp mirin
2 tbsp sweet white miso paste
2 frozen salmon fillets, thawed and
    chopped into large chunks
sea salt

Put a pan of water on to boil for the noodles.

In another saucepan, heat the oil over a low–medium heat, add the garlic and ginger and cook for 2 minutes. Add the spring onion whites and mushrooms to the pan, turn the heat up to high and cook for another 5 minutes, until the mushrooms are wilted and most of the water has evaporated (frozen mushrooms will let out a lot of water).

Meanwhile, add the noodles to the saucepan of boiling water and cook according to the packet instructions.

Add the carrots and the hot stock to the mushroom pan and cook for another 5 minutes, or until the carrots are almost tender. Add the edamame and sweetcorn, bring back to a gentle simmer and cook for another minute.

Stir in the mirin and miso, then add the chunks of salmon and most of the spring onion greens. Simmer very gently for 2–3 minutes until the salmon is just cooked.

Drain the noodles and tip them into the broth. Season to taste with salt. Stir everything together, then divide between two bowls and sprinkle with the reserved spring onion greens to serve.

Freezer adaptation:
You don't have to use the vegetables listed here. Feel free to tweak the varieties and quantities of veg to what you have in the freezer.

Will it re-freeze?
Yes, but the noodles will be a little mushy. Best to prepare it fresh as it's so quick to whip up.

Serves 2
–
Prep 10 mins
–
Cook 20 mins

Fish

FISH, DILL & ROAST POTATO PIE P

Packets of frozen seafood mixes are a cost-effective way to enjoy fish, and if you have a bag of roasties in the freezer, these can be used to replace the classic mash. Granted, it's a little more indulgent, but I doubt you'll hear many complaints. I recommend defrosting the seafood first, but if it's still frozen, just heat it in the sauce on the hob a little longer until it's defrosted, adding a splash more milk, if needs be.

600g (1lb 5oz) frozen roast potatoes
40g (1½oz/3 tbsp) butter
30g (1oz/4 tbsp) plain (all-purpose) flour
400ml (14fl oz/1¾ cups) milk
650g (1lb 7oz) frozen fish pie mix, defrosted
finely grated zest of ½ lemon
a large handful of dill, chopped
sea salt flakes and ground black pepper

Preheat the oven to 220°C/425°F/gas mark 7.

Put the frozen roast potatoes in a roasting pan and roast for about 40 minutes until golden and crisp, or as per the packet instructions.

About 10 minutes before the end of the potatoes' cooking time, melt the butter in a saucepan over low–medium heat. Add the flour and cook for a few minutes to cook out the flavour of the flour. Add the milk, a little at a time, whisking to get rid of any lumps. Cook for a few minutes until the sauce starts to thicken, then add the fish. Stir into the sauce and heat for a couple of minutes until it starts to cook, then turn off the heat and add the lemon zest and dill. Season to taste with salt and pepper.

By now, the potatoes should be ready. Remove them from the oven and transfer them to a chopping board. Turn the oven down to 180°C/350°F/gas mark 4. Using a potato masher, flatten each roast potato until it bursts and starts to let out the soft flesh inside, but is still just about in one piece.

Tip the fish filling into a baking dish. Layer the potatoes on top, arranging them in a circular pattern if you are feeling artistic, or just spread them in a relatively even layer. Sprinkle the top of the pie with salt flakes.

Return the dish to the oven for 20–25 minutes, until the sauce is piping hot and bubbling and the potatoes are even more golden and crispy.

Will it re-freeze?

Yes, but don't do the final bake. Cook the sauce and stir in the fish. Roast and crush the potatoes and assemble it in freezer-safe baking dishes (or foil trays). Freeze like that as a homemade ready meal, then let defrost and cook for 30–40 minutes in the oven at 180°C/350°F/gas mark 4, or until piping hot throughout. If there are two of you, you could always cook off half straight away and keep two portions in the freezer for a day when you don't have much time to prep.

Serves 4
–
Prep 20 mins
–
Cook 1 hour

SALMON & SPINACH KOULIABAC P

This is a form of wellington, made almost entirely from frozen and store-cupboard ingredients, and is no less impressive for that. You will need thick strips of salmon fillet (rather than any flatter fillets from the tail end of the fish), if you want to shape the lovely ridges across the top of the kouliabac.

250g (9oz) frozen spinach
40g (1½oz/3 tbsp) butter
200g (7oz) frozen diced onion
   (or 1 onion, finely diced)
1 tbsp frozen chopped garlic (or 2 fresh
   cloves, finely chopped)
a good pinch of ground allspice
140g (5oz) cooked basmati rice (from
   a ready-cooked pouch is fine)
3 tbsp frozen (or fresh) chopped
   parsley
a small bunch of dill, chopped
finely grated zest of 1 lemon
1 × 375g (13oz) ready-rolled frozen
   puff pastry sheet
4 frozen salmon fillets, defrosted and
   skin removed
1 egg, beaten
sea salt and ground black pepper
roasted cherry tomatoes or cooked
   freezer veg, to serve

Will it re-freeze?

Yes, you could re-freeze this in individual portions for convenience, then reheat gently in the oven, wrapped in foil at first, then removing the foil to crisp up the pastry for the last few minutes.

Cook the spinach in the microwave for 1–2 minutes to just defrost and break up the lumps.

Melt the butter in a large saucepan and add the onion. Cook for 8 minutes until softened and translucent. Add the garlic and allspice and cook for another couple of minutes, then add the spinach. Cook, breaking up the lumps a bit more with a spatula, until the spinach is well incorporated, then add the rice. Stir in, then turn off the heat and stir in the herbs and lemon zest too. Season well with salt and pepper and allow the mixture to cool completely.

Once the mixture is cool, preheat the oven to 190°C/375°F/ gas mark 5. Unroll the pastry sheet and spoon the spinach filling onto the sheet, arranging it in a line down one long side of the sheet, leaving a 1cm (½in) gap and the ends bare to seal. Arrange the salmon fillets over the mixture in diagonal lines crossing the mound of rice filling, then brush the edges of the pastry sheet with a little of the beaten egg. Tuck in the ends of the pastry, as if wrapping a present, then fold the clear side of the pastry over the filling and seal along one side. Make several diagonal cuts across the top of the pastry, between the salmon fillets, then brush the whole thing with beaten egg to glaze. Chill in the fridge for 30 minutes.

Bake the kouliabac for about 35 minutes, or until the pastry is puffed and golden and the salmon is just cooked. This is lovely served with roasted tomatoes, or just delve into the freezer for some more veg options.

Serves 4
–
Prep 20 mins
–
Cook 50 mins

FREEZER FEAST: SEAFOOD PAELLA

Most of the ingredients for this can come out of either your freezer or store cupboard. Frozen seafood, chicken and veg are all combined with fragrant paella rice to create this flexible feast; leave out the chicken, sub in beans for the peas, or use whatever seafood you have to hand. It will all taste delicious.

2 tbsp olive oil, plus extra for frying the seafood
100g (3½oz) chorizo, sliced into 3–4mm (⅛in) thick slices
1 large chicken breast, chopped into bite-sized pieces
40g (1½oz/3 tbsp) butter
250g (9oz) frozen diced onion (or 1 large onion, finely diced)
1 tbsp chopped frozen garlic (or 2 fresh cloves, finely chopped)
1½ tsp sweet smoked paprika
a generous pinch of saffron threads
250g (9oz) paella rice (such as Calasparra)
150ml (5fl oz/scant ⅔ cup) good white wine
700ml (24fl oz/3 cups) chicken stock
4 large tomatoes, deseeded and diced
300g (10½oz) frozen squid rings, defrosted
300g (10½oz) large shell-on king prawns (jumbo shrimp), defrosted
175g (6oz) frozen peppers
120g (4¼oz) frozen peas
sea salt and ground black pepper
chopped fresh or frozen parsley, to serve
lemon wedges, to serve

Heat the oil in a large frying pan over medium–high heat and add the chorizo. Cook for a couple of minutes until the oil comes out of the chorizo, then remove from the pan with a slotted spoon, leaving the oil in the pan. Add the chicken pieces and cook until they are browned all over. Turn the heat down to low–medium, add the butter, onion, garlic and paprika, and return the chorizo to the pan. Cook for about 8 minutes until the onion is translucent and soft. Meanwhile, put the saffron threads in a small bowl and add about 3 tbsp warm water.

Add the rice to the pan and stir it around to coat it in the flavoursome oil, then add the white wine and saffron, along with it's soaking liquid, and cook until almost all the liquid has been absorbed by the rice. Add three-quarters of the chicken stock and the tomatoes and cook for about 15 minutes, or until the rice is almost cooked. Keep an eye on the pan as it cooks, and if it looks like it is beginning to catch, add a splash more of the remaining stock.

While the rice is cooking, heat a drizzle of olive oil in a large non-stick frying pan over a high heat and fry the squid rings in two batches for a couple of minutes until browning. Set aside. Add another drizzle of oil to the pan and fry the prawns – again in two batches so you don't overcrowd the pan – until golden on the outside.

Once the rice is almost cooked, stir the peppers and peas into the paella, then add the seafood. Cook the paella for another few minutes until the rice and vegetables are fully cooked and the prawns have finished cooking in the centres.

Taste and season with salt and pepper, then sprinkle the paella with chopped parsley and squeeze over a little lemon juice. Serve in the pan with more lemon wedges on the side.

Will it re-freeze?

Yes, although it is best eaten fresh. Rice tends to go a little mushy when it's frozen, so a defrosted, reheated version will be a shadow of its former self, but still edible and tasty nonetheless.

Serves 4
–
Prep 20 mins
–
Cook 40 mins

FISH PARCELS WITH FREEZER BUTTER & PARMA HAM

These fish 'Kiev'-style parcels are based on the chicken classic, and make use of fabulous freezer butters, which can be on standby to add flavour where needed. Use whichever flavoured freezer butter you fancy for these from the recipes on page 11. Serve with frozen fries and green freezer veg or a salad. You could also use the butters for a chicken version, if you like.

8 thin and reasonably flat frozen fish fillets (such as pollock), defrosted
8 slices frozen Lemon and Herb or Smoked Anchovy Butter (see page 11)
12–16 slices Parma ham (prosciutto)
skin-on fries, to serve
salad or green freezer veg, to serve

Preheat the oven to 190°C/375°F/gas mark 5.

Lay out a long slice of fish on a chopping board and place a slice of the butter at the narrowest end. Roll up the fish so you have a parcel, with the butter in the middle and the seam underneath, then place it on a piece of Parma ham, arranging it so that the spiral of the fish roll will be covered by ham and seal in the butter. Wrap the ham around the parcel to seal it, then wrap with another slice going in the other direction to keep the butter in. Repeat to wrap all of the parcels.

Place the fish parcels on a baking tray and bake in the preheated oven for about 15 minutes, or until the ham is crisping up and the fish is cooked through.

Serve the fish parcels with skin on fries and salad or veg, drizzled with any flavoured butter that may have escaped onto the baking tray.

Freezer adaptation:

Go traditional and use the freezer butters with chicken breast fillets instead to make something more akin to the original Kiev. If you have breadcrumbs in the freezer too, use these (after a coat of flour, then beaten egg) to coat the chicken rather than the ham.

Will it re-freeze?

Yes, these will freeze. I recommend allowing the parcels to defrost naturally, then reheating gently in the microwave.

Serves 4
–
Prep 15 mins
–
Cook 15 mins

ZA'ATAR FISH WITH HERBY QUINOA & BABY BROAD BEAN SALAD P

This is a simple way to zhuzh up basic frozen white fish fillets, inspired by the flavours of the Middle East. Serve with a herby tabbouleh-style salad, using frozen baby broad beans and pomegranate seeds – both now found in the freezer aisle – or use fresh equivalents.

4 frozen white fish fillets, defrosted (or use a couple each if they are very small)
2 tsp za'atar
finely grated zest of 1 lemon (save the juice for the salad)
olive oil, for frying

For the salad
100g (3½oz) quinoa
250g (9oz) frozen baby broad (fava) beans
juice of 1 lemon
2–3 tbsp olive oil (to taste)
a very large bunch of fresh parsley, roughly chopped
150g (5½oz) cherry tomatoes, quartered
6 spring onions (scallions), sliced
a small handful of (fresh or frozen) pomegranate seeds
sea salt and ground black pepper

Freezer adaptation:
You can use standard broad beans for this rather than baby ones, but you may want to peel them. Equally, frozen peas or edamame beans will also work in place of broad beans.

Will it re-freeze?
The fish will re-freeze once cooked if you have leftovers, but the salad should be enjoyed fresh.

Lay the defrosted fish fillets out in a shallow dish and sprinkle over the za'atar, making sure the fillets are seasoned on both sides. Grate over the lemon zest and cover the dish with clingfilm (plastic wrap). Leave to marinate for an hour or so in the fridge – but you can leave this for longer, if you wish.

Meanwhile, cook the quinoa as per the packet instructions, then leave to cool.

Blanch the baby broad beans for 2 minutes until defrosted and just cooked and leave these to cool too. There's no need to double pod these, as baby beans should have quite tender skins, but if you are using standard frozen broad beans, you may wish to remove the tougher pale outer skin.

In a small bowl, combine the lemon juice and olive oil for the salad dressing. Taste and season well with salt and pepper.

Just before serving, add the quinoa to a large bowl along with the broad beans, parsley, tomatoes and spring onions. Drizzle over the dressing and toss everything together.

Pour a little olive oil into a large non-stick frying pan and fry the fish fillets for a couple of minutes on each side, until turning lightly golden and just cooked through.

Divide the salad between four serving plates and top with the fried fish. Finish with a sprinkling of pomegranate seeds.

Serves 4
–
Prep 15 mins
–
Cook 6 mins

Fish

CARBS

Carbs provide the vital stodge element to dishes magicked up from freezer provisions. While they feature heavily in the other chapters, too, here they are the stars. Yorkshire puddings are repurposed to make delicious sticky toffee date treats, frozen bread is revived in French Toast and a rustic Italian Ribbolita soup, and classics such as tortillas and a breakfast hash are reinvented with frozen potatoes relieving you of the hard work. And not forgetting pastry, the mainstay of pleasing party spreads; serve up pastry straws flavoured with three different freezer seasonings.

WAFFLEY SPANISH TORTILLA v

Using waffles in a tortilla may very well appal many Spanish cooks, but it does make the perfect brunch after the night before. Sticking a few waffles in the oven is far easier than peeling and slicing potato and attending to it while it fries leisurely in the pan, and the waffles give it that greasy spoon feel that is an essential ingredient in a hangover aid.

4 frozen potato waffles
2 tbsp olive oil
1 small onion, finely sliced
    (or 150g/5½oz frozen
    diced onion)
6 large eggs
sea salt and ground black pepper
mayo, aioli, ketchup or dip of your
    choice, to serve

Preheat the oven to 200°C/400°F/gas mark 6.

Place the frozen waffles on a baking tray and bake for 15–18 minutes until crisp and golden brown.

Meanwhile, heat the oil in a 24cm/9½in (at the rim) heavy-based non-stick frying pan with a heatproof handle. Add the onion and cook over a low–medium heat for a good 10 minutes until very soft and melting. Tip them onto a plate and set aside.

Once the waffles are ready, remove them from the oven and turn on the grill (broiler) to high. Place two of the waffles in the pan, then halve the other two and arrange them around the sides to line the pan. Tip the onion back into the pan and spread evenly over the waffles.

Beat the eggs together and season well with salt and pepper. Tip them into the pan and cover with a lid. Place over a low–medium heat for about 8 minutes, until the base of the tortilla is well cooked.

Transfer the pan to the preheated grill and cook for another 3–4 minutes, or until the top is cooked and golden.

Using oven gloves, as the pan and handle will be very hot, place a plate on top of the pan, then invert the pan and plate together to turn the tortilla out onto the plate.

Slice the tortilla into wedges and serve hot with whatever condiment you fancy.

Freezer adaptation:

You could add in any small freezer veg that you have (peas, sweetcorn, etc.), as long as you defrost it and dry on kitchen paper first.

Will it re-freeze?:

Yes. Let it defrost naturally, then warm it up in the oven or microwave.

Serves 2–4
–
Prep 10 mins
–
Cook 30 mins

HASH-BROWN & HAM HASH WITH FREEZER VEGGIES

This weekend brunch is great for using up the broken bits at the bottom of the hash brown bag, as you are going to chop them up anyway. The veg can be mixed and matched in whatever way you like – just make sure it is all quite small (or in small pieces) so it cooks evenly. Ham ends are one of my freezer essentials (see page 8), and are great to chuck into throw-together dishes like this.

12 frozen hash browns
300g (10½oz) 'small' freezer veg (such as peas, sweetcorn, bags of mixed veg with chopped carrots, peppers, green beans, etc.)
3 tbsp olive oil
1 red or white onion, finely sliced
1 tbsp chopped frozen garlic (or 2 fresh cloves, finely chopped)
leaves from 2 sprigs thyme, or ½ tsp dried
300g (10½oz) frozen ham ends, defrosted
1½ tbsp Worcestershire sauce
4 eggs
sea salt and ground black pepper

Freezer adaptation:

If you don't have any ham ends in the freezer, you could just use a can of corned beef, as is classic.

Will it re-freeze?

The egg won't be too pleasant, but the rest of it should freeze just fine. Simply defrost and reheat in the microwave.

Start by preheating the oven and baking the hash browns according to the instructions on the packet.

Put the frozen veg into a bowl and cover with a kettle of boiling water. Leave them for a few minutes to defrost, then tip them into a colander and let drain and cool.

Once the hash browns are cooked, chop them up into rough chunks and set aside.

Heat 2 tbsp of the olive oil in a large frying pan or sauté pan, preferably non-stick, over a low–medium heat. Add the onion and cook for about 5–6 minutes until softened and turning translucent. Add the garlic and thyme and cook for another 3–4 minutes. Raise the heat to medium–high and add the ham. Cook for a couple of minutes until the meat is browning a little, then tip in the drained veg and the hash browns. Measure in the Worcestershire sauce and season with salt and pepper. Continue to cook for another couple of minutes until everything is warmed through, stirring frequently so that nothing starts to catch on the bottom of the pan.

Meanwhile, heat the remaining 1 tbsp of oil in another non-stick frying pan and fry the eggs for a few minutes until the whites are set but the yolks are still runny.

Divide the hash between four plates and top each one with a fried egg to serve.

Serves 4
–
Prep 10 mins
–
Cook 35 mins

Carbs

LEMON RICOTTA STUFFED FRENCH TOAST WITH BLUEBERRY SAUCE v

This is a great recipe for rescuing bread that has been kicking around the freezer a little too long – giving bread a new life was the traditional function of what the French call *pain perdue* or 'lost bread'. Not only does it use up old bread, but you can make a delicious accompanying sauce from a bag of frozen blueberries.

8 slices frozen bread, defrosted
4 large eggs
200ml (7fl oz/scant 1 cup) milk
200g (7oz) ricotta
finely grated zest of 1 lemon
1½ tbsp icing (confectioner's) sugar, plus extra to dust
unsalted butter, for cooking

For the sauce
250g (9oz) frozen blueberries
2 tbsp icing (confectioner's) sugar
freshly squeezed juice of ½ lemon (use the one you have zested for the filling)

Freezer adaptation:

You can use any bags of berries you have in the freezer – they don't have to be blueberries, although they do go well with the lemony filling. You also don't have to go to the trouble of stuffing the bread with ricotta, if you don't want to. Simply follow the recipe and cook the slices separately and serve with the berry sauce – it will still be delicious.

Will it re-freeze?

I wouldn't recommend it for this. These are definitely best cooked fresh.

Serves 4
–
Prep 10 mins
–
Cook 40 mins

Lay the bread slices out in a single layer in a shallow dish (or two). In a jug, beat together the eggs and milk, then pour it all over the bread slices. Turn them over in the mixture to make sure they are all evenly coated, then leave them for 10–15 minutes for the egg to completely soak in.

Meanwhile, make the filling for the toast by beating together the ricotta, lemon zest and icing sugar until smooth.

To make the sauce, put the blueberries in a saucepan with the icing sugar and lemon juice. Cook over a gentle heat until the berries have defrosted and let out their juice, and that juice has begun to thicken again. You can leave the pan over a gentle heat while you cook the toast, stirring occasionally.

By now, the bread should have absorbed all of the egg mixture. Divide the lemony filling between four of the bread slices, spreading it out over the slices but leaving a 1cm (½in) clear border around the edge. Top those four slices with the remaining bread to make ricotta sandwiches.

Melt a little butter in a non-stick frying pan over low–medium heat and add one of the sandwiches to the pan. Leave the sandwich to cook for 3–4 minutes, or until the bottom of the bread is a golden colour. Press down gently with a spatula to flatten and seal the sandwich as it cooks. Once the sandwich is golden, flip it over and cook for the same amount of time on the other side.

Dust the top of the sandwich with a little icing sugar (try and keep it on the bread and not in the pan or it will burn). Flip it over and cook for 20–30 seconds until it has melted. Dust the other side, flip and cook again for a few seconds until you have a caramelized crust on both sides.

Remove the sandwich from the pan, slice it in half diagonally and top with a little blueberry sauce to serve. Give the pan a quick wipe with a piece of kitchen paper and repeat the process until all the sandwiches are cooked. There's no call for courtesy here – eat them hot and fresh out the pan rather than waiting until all the sandwiches are cooked – they are much better that way.

STICKY TOFFEE DATE YORKIES v

These treats are based on the popovers, filled with mincemeat, we were fed as kids. A basic batter used for Yorkshire puddings can also be used here, but ready-made Yorkies speed things up a little, cut down on washing up, and are a great way to repurpose any you may have lurking in the freezer, if a Sunday roast isn't imminent.

200g (7oz) soft pitted dates, sliced
2 tbsp vanilla extract
50g (1¾oz/3½ tbsp) butter
50g (1¾oz/¼ cup) dark soft
    brown sugar
100ml (3½fl oz/scant ½ cup) double
    (heavy) cream
12 frozen Yorkshire puddings

Preheat the oven to 200°C/400°F/gas mark 6.

Start by making the sticky toffee filling. Put the dates in a saucepan with 4 tbsp of water and the vanilla extract, and cook over a low heat, covered, for about 4 minutes until the dates have softened.

Add the butter and sugar to the pan and let them melt into the mixture, then add the cream and stir in. Still over a low heat, cook the filling for about 10 minutes, stirring frequently, until it starts to thicken to a scoopable consistency, being very careful not to let it burn. Remove the pan from the heat.

Arrange your Yorkies in a 12-hole muffin pan, so they stay upright and the filling doesn't escape. Divide the date mixture evenly between the Yorkshires and bake for about 6 minutes, or until the puddings are heated through and crisp and the mixture is hot and forming a crust on top.

Allow to cool a little before eating, as the filling will be as hot as molten lava.

Will it re-freeze?

Not really, but they won't last more than a few minutes once served, anyway.

Makes 12
–
Prep 10 mins
–
Cook 20 mins

Carbs

VOL-AU-VENTS

Retro, of course, but who doesn't secretly love these? Apparently someone is still buying them, as most supermarkets will have a stack of vol-au-vent pastry tucked away in the freezer aisle. While party guests may mock, you'll probably still find them hovering by the buffet table, hoovering up these along with the spines of the cheese and pineapple hedgehog. But what to put in them?

a packet of 18 frozen vol-au-vent cases
whatever fillings you wish (see opposite for suggestions)

Savoury:

• Use the spiced chickpea and leek filling from the pancakes on page 97.

• Use the mushroom, red wine and thyme filling from page 106. Cook the ragù down so that it is quite thick, then fill the vol-au-vents and top with a grating of Parmesan and a fresh thyme sprig to decorate.

• Use the cheese sauce from the gratin on page 105. Let it cool and thicken, then stir in whatever you fancy – I like chunks of ham and cooked peas.

• Use either of the dips on page 90 – pea and mint or spiced butternut would both be delicious, but not in the same case!

• Fill with the BBQ beef filling from page 14 and top with a dollop of soured cream and a sprig of coriander (cilantro).

Sweet:

• Use a little of the cheesecake mixture from page 130 and top with defrosted frozen berries.

• Spoon in a little chocolate sauce (see page 11) and top with a dollop of cream and defrosted frozen cherries.

• Use the coconut cream with mango and pineapple filling from the meringue cake on page 128. Top with desiccated (dried shredded) coconut.

• Stuff sticky toffee date goo (see page 72) into vol-au-vents instead of Yorkshire puds.

Makes 18
(or as many
as your event
requires)

Carbs

FREEZER FEAST: PASTRY PARTY STRAWS v

These treats make use of a few key freezer and pantry ingredients. I freeze small tubs of store-bought miso and harissa in two-tablespoon portions, and slightly larger portions for homemade pesto (see page 11). The main problem with frozen rolled pastry is that it often cracks when you unroll it; to avoid this, make sure it's not too cold when you start working with it.

Miso Sesame Straws

a sheet of frozen ready-rolled puff
    pastry, defrosted
4 tbsp white miso paste
3 tbsp sesame seeds
1 egg, beaten

Harissa Almond Straws

a sheet of frozen ready-rolled puff
    pastry, defrosted
2–3 tbsp harissa (depending how hot
    you want them)
1 egg, beaten
50g (1¾oz) blanched almonds, finely
    chopped
sea salt flakes

Cheesy Pesto Straws

a sheet of frozen ready-rolled puff
    pastry, defrosted
5 tbsp Pesto Genovese (see page 11)
1 egg, beaten
25g (1oz) Parmesan, finely grated

Line two large baking sheets with baking parchment. Unroll the pastry sheet and follow the guides for whichever recipe you are making below:

For the miso sesame straws – spread the miso paste all over the pastry sheet, then sprinkle evenly with half of the sesame seeds. Once you have twisted and glazed the strips (see below), sprinkle over the other half of the sesame seeds.

For the harissa almond straws – spread the harissa all over the pastry sheet. Once you have twisted and glazed the strips (see below), sprinkle over the finely chopped almonds and some flaky sea salt.

For the cheesy pesto straws – spread the pesto all over the pastry sheet. Once you have twisted and glazed the strips (see below), sprinkle over the grated Parmesan.

Once you have spread your choice of filling over the sheet, cut the sheet widthways into 2cm (¾in) wide strips. Hold a strip by one end and, using the other hand, twist the other end to form a spiral. Place on the prepared baking sheet and repeat to twist the remaining strips. Place the trays in the fridge to chill for 30 minutes. Meanwhile, preheat the oven to 190°C/375°F/gas mark 5

Glaze all the exposed (unfilled) pastry with the beaten egg, then sprinkle with whatever your recipe of choice requires.

Bake the straws for 15–18 minutes, until puffed up and golden. Serve warm.

Will it re-freeze?

Best to make these ones fresh.

> **Makes 18**
> –
> **Prep 10 mins**
> –
> **Cook 18 mins**

Carbs

LOADED LATTICE FRIES V

I think we can all agree that frozen lattice fries are a bit of an indulgence, but piling them high with smashed beans and freshly made guacamole and salsa does give them a nutritional boost, and makes a deliciously colourful platter for feeding a crowd. If you want to make this vegan, simply use a plant-based cheese.

500g (1lb 2oz) frozen lattice fries

For the refried beans
1 tbsp olive oil
¾ red onion, finely diced (save the remaining ¼ for the pico de gallo)
1 tsp ground cumin
1 tbsp chopped frozen garlic (or 2 fresh cloves, finely chopped)
1 tbsp frozen (or fresh) chopped red chilli
1 × 400g (14oz) can pinto beans or black beans, drained and rinsed
freshly squeezed juice of ½ lime
sea salt and ground black pepper

For the pico de gallo
¼ red onion, finely diced
2 large ripe tomatoes, deseeded and finely diced
a small handful of fresh coriander (cilantro) leaves, chopped (or 1 tbsp frozen chopped coriander)
1 tsp frozen (or fresh) chopped chilli
freshly squeezed juice of ½ lime

To serve
1 x recipe quantity Freezer Guacamole (see page 50)
sliced jalapeños
grated Cheddar or Monterey Jack cheese
finely sliced spring onions (scallions)

Preheat the oven to 220°C/425°F/gas mark 7, or to whatever the instructions on your lattice fries packet state.

Start by making the beans, as they will sit for a little while. Heat the oil in a non-stick frying pan over a low heat and add the onion, cumin, garlic and chilli. Cook for a good 8 minutes until the onion is well softened. Add the beans and cook for another 5 minutes or so, mashing the beans a little as they cook so you get a chunky puréed texture. Squeeze in the lime juice and season well with salt and pepper.

Spread the lattice fries out on an oven tray and bake according to the packet instructions.

Meanwhile, make the pico de gallo by combining all the ingredients in a small bowl. Make your guacamole now too, according to page 50, if you haven't already. Gently rewarm the beans, if you need to.

To serve, pile the fries onto a serving platter and top with dollops of the beans and the guacamole. (You don't have to add it all – serve any extra on the side.) Sprinkle over the pico de gallo, jalapeños, cheese and spring onions.

Will it re-freeze?
The beans will freeze alone if you have any left over, but the fresh salsa and guacamole won't survive very well.

Serves 4
–
Prep 15 mins
–
Cook 40 mins

ROAST PATATAS BRAVAS VE

The Spanish classic patatas bravas can be churned out so easily if you have a bag of roasties in the freezer. The frozen variety generally have a lot of basting fats in the coating, and so produce something that's practically fried. Team this with the tortilla on page 66 and some Spanish cured meats and salad for a respectable spread in no time at all.

600g (1lb 5oz) frozen roast potatoes (ensure they are vegan, if necessary)
1 tbsp olive oil
150g (5½oz) frozen chopped onion (or 1 small onion, finely diced)
1 tbsp chopped frozen garlic (or 2 fresh cloves, finely chopped)
1½ tbsp frozen (or fresh) chopped chilli
1 × 400g (14oz) can chopped tomatoes
1 tbsp tomato purée (paste)
2 tsp sugar
2 tsp hot smoked paprika
sea salt and ground black pepper

Preheat the oven to 220°C/425°F/gas mark 7 and cook the roast potatoes as per the packet instructions.

Meanwhile, to make the sauce, heat the oil in a small saucepan over a low–medium heat and fry the onion for 5 minutes until softening. Add the garlic and chilli and cook for another couple of minutes before adding the chopped tomatoes, tomato purée, sugar and smoked paprika. Cook the sauce for about 20 minutes until reduced and thickened. Taste and season with salt and pepper.

Chop the potatoes into cubes if large, or just leave whole, if smaller. Pile them into a tapas serving dish and trickle over some of the hot sauce. Serve the rest of the sauce on the side so people can be as brave as they dare.

Freezer adaptation:

If you don't have roast potatoes, you could do a version of patatas bravas with most freezer potato products: chips (fries), waffles (cut up), hash browns, curly fries, you name it.

Will it re-freeze?

The sauce freezes well, and is good to have as a freezer standby, as it will work as a pizza or pasta sauce too.

Serves 4
–
Prep 10 mins
–
Cook 25 mins

Carbs

RIBBOLITA v

Freezing pre-sliced bread ensures that toast is never more than a couple of minutes away, and the bread stays much fresher than if left in the bread bin. But if you're anything like me and head straight for the fluffy middle of the loaf, you often end up with bags of bread crusts in the freezer. This Tuscan bread soup is a great way to use them up, as the more crusty bits hold their own for longer in the liquid.

2 tbsp olive oil, plus extra for drizzling
1 large onion, finely sliced (or 200g/7oz frozen diced onion)
3 celery sticks, sliced
200g (7oz) frozen sliced carrots (frozen small chantenay carrots work too, or use 2 peeled and sliced fresh carrots)
2 tbsp frozen chopped garlic (or 4 fresh cloves, finely chopped)
2 × 400g (14oz) cans chopped tomatoes
500ml (17fl oz/2 cups) vegetable stock
2 tbsp tomato purée (paste)
2 sprigs frozen (or fresh) rosemary
2 sprigs frozen (or fresh) thyme
1 tsp dried sage
a chunk of frozen Parmesan rind (see page 10, optional)
1 × 400g (14oz) can cannellini beans, drained and rinsed
200g (7oz) frozen Savoy cabbage
6 slices stale bread, or small heels of bread
sea salt and ground black pepper
Pesto Genovese (see page 11) and/or freshly grated Parmesan, to serve

Heat the oil in a large saucepan over a low heat and add the onion, celery, carrots and garlic. Cook gently for about 10 minutes until everything has softened.

Add the tomatoes and stock to the pan along with the tomato purée, rosemary, thyme, sage and Parmesan rind. Leave the soup to cook for about 20 minutes, or until the veggies are all tender, then stir in the beans. Add the cabbage and let it just wilt in the pan for a couple of minutes (frozen cabbage will already be quite softened), then taste and season with salt and pepper.

Rip or slice the bread into chunks and pop it into the bottom of the soup bowls. Ladle the soup over the top (scooping out the Parmesan rind if you find it along the way) and leave for a couple of minutes for the soup to soften the bread, then stir everything together. Serve the soup topped with generous dollops of pesto.

Will it re-freeze?

Yes, this is a good one for batch freezing. Freeze in individual portions (including the bread) and you will have a complete meal to pop in your bag in the morning and take with you.

Serves 4–6
–
Prep 15 mins
–
Cook 35 mins

Carbs

FROZEN PAIN AU CHOCOLAT PUDDING v

A take on the bread and butter pudding, only more indulgent. You'll need about 6 or 7 pastries, depending on how big they are. You can, of course, do this with any other fresh pastries you have kicking around, but as this uses freezer and store-cupboard ingredients, it makes a simple pudding that you can probably knock up without a trip to the shops.

6–7 frozen pain au chocolat pastries
butter, for greasing
chocolate chips or raisins (optional)
200ml (7fl oz/scant 1 cup) double (heavy) cream
200ml (7fl oz/scant 1 cup) whole milk
125g (4½oz) caster (superfine) sugar, plus extra for sprinkling
3 large egg yolks
ice cream, to serve (optional)

Cook the pain au chocolat according to the packet instructions and let them cool fully. Once cool, cut them into thick slices and set aside for them to stale slightly.

Preheat the oven to 180°C/350°F/gas mark 4 and grease a baking dish well with butter.

Arrange the pastry slices into the baking dish in two layers, sprinkling in any additions you'd like between the layers and making it look neat on top. Don't worry if it doesn't come right to the top of the dish; it should rise up a little as it cooks. Set aside.

Put the cream, milk and sugar in a saucepan over a medium heat and, stirring, warm it to dissolve the sugar, but don't let it boil. Meanwhile, whisk the egg yolks in a bowl. Once the cream is warm, pour it onto the egg yolks, whisking all the time as you do, until everything is well combined.

Pour the custard over the pastries in the baking dish, making sure you leave a bit of the pastry protruding out the top of the liquid for some nice crispy bits. Leave the pudding for 10 minutes or so for the custard to soak into the pastries a bit.

Sprinkle the top of the pudding with a little more sugar, then transfer the dish to the oven and bake for about 30 minutes, or until the custard is set and the top of the pudding is golden and crispy.

Serve straight out the oven, topped with a ball of ice cream, if you like.

Freezer adaptation:

Pain au chocolat are the best, in my opinion (and remove the need for any inclusions, like chocolate chips or raisins), but you could use plain croissants, almond croissants or raisin pastries, too – whatever you have in the freezer.

Will it re-freeze?

Yes, although I would be surprised if there's any left to freeze.

Serves 6
–
Prep 10 mins
–
Cook 1 hour

VEG

The options for what you can make with the staggering variety of frozen veggies now available are limitless. Simple post-work dinners, such as Green Bean and Halloumi Masala or Mushroom and Pepper Stroganoff, provide a fuss-free way of getting closer to your five a day. For something a little fancy, give the Honeyed Carrot and Rosemary Tarte Tatin a go – it's really not as tricky as you'd think – or the Risotto (pictured here), which can be adapted to use anything green that's hiding out in your freezer.

MEXICAN CHARRED CORN CHOWDER v

Sweetcorn has always been one of my favourite soups – but add a charred smoky flavour to it, as well as a kick of spice, and it takes on a far more interesting flavour, whilst retaining all of its comfort-food credentials. If you want to make this vegan, simply omit the butter and use a little more oil.

600g (1lb 5oz) frozen sweetcorn
30g (1oz/2 tbsp) butter
1 tbsp olive oil
12–14 spring onions (scallions), finely sliced, white and green parts separated
1 tsp dried ancho chilli flakes, plus extra to sprinkle
1 tsp Mexican oregano (or standard oregano)
¼ tsp ground cumin
1 litre (35fl oz/4 cups) hot vegetable or chicken stock
sea salt and ground black pepper

Tip 100g (3½oz) of the sweetcorn into a colander and run warm water over it to defrost. Drain well, then tip onto kitchen paper to dry out completely.

Heat a large frying pan over a very high heat and add the dried sweetcorn. Cook for a few minutes until the corn is beginning to char and blacken in places. This will probably smoke a bit, so have your extractor on or a window open! Once blackened, turn off the heat and set aside.

Melt the butter in a large saucepan with the oil and add the spring onion whites. Sauté for a couple of minutes until the onion whites are softened, then add the chilli flakes, oregano and cumin to the pan and cook for a minute or so longer until smelling aromatic.

Add the hot stock to the saucepan, along with the remaining, still-frozen sweetcorn. Return the liquid to a boil, then simmer for 10 minutes, or until the sweetcorn is very tender. Add about three quarters of the charred sweetcorn and most of the spring onion greens and continue to cook for another few minutes to warm the corn through and wilt the greens.

Use a stick blender to blitz the soup until everything is puréed but it still has a bit of texture. Season to taste with salt and pepper, then divide between four bowls. Sprinkle the top of each bowl with a little charred corn, a few spring onion greens and a few more chilli flakes, and serve.

Will it re-freeze?

Yes, this is a great one for the freezer. Allow to defrost and rewarm gently in a saucepan, or pop in the microwave straight from frozen.

Serves 4
–
Prep 10 mins
–
Cook 20 mins

FREEZER VEG DIP DOUBLE

These two veg-heavy dips almost offer a spring and an autumn option, but are also lovely served together – the rich, sweet butternut a foil for the fresh spring peas. Serve with crackers or crudités for dipping.

Pea, Feta and Mint Dip V

200g (7oz) frozen peas
2 spring onions (scallions), finely sliced
1 tbsp freshly squeezed lemon juice
1 tbsp extra virgin olive oil
a large handful of mint leaves, plus a
     few small leaves to serve
80g (2¾oz) feta cheese
sea salt and ground black pepper

Spiced Butternut Dip VE

300g (10½oz) frozen butternut
     squash cubes
2 tbsp olive oil
½ tsp dried thyme
½ tsp ground cumin
¼ tsp ground cinnamon
¼ tsp cayenne pepper
½ tsp sea salt flakes, plus extra to taste
1 large garlic clove, unpeeled
1 tbsp freshly squeezed lemon juice
sea salt and ground black pepper
30g (1oz) hazelnuts, toasted and
     crushed, to serve

Pea, Feta and Mint Dip

Blanch the frozen peas in boiling salted water for 3 minutes, or until just tender. Tip into a sieve (strainer) and run under cold water immediately to cool them down and stop them cooking. Leave to drain.

Put the peas in a food processor with the spring onions, lemon juice, olive oil and mint leaves. Blitz until the mixture is smooth-ish, but a little texture is good. Tip the purée into a bowl, crumble in the cheese and stir together. Taste and season with salt and pepper, then serve garnished with an extra sprinkle of black pepper and a few small mint leaves.

Spiced Butternut Dip

Preheat the oven to 200°C/400°F/gas mark 6.

Weigh the butternut into a bowl and break up if all frozen into a big lump. Add the olive oil, thyme, spices, salt and garlic clove and stir to combine well. Tip the lot onto a baking tray and roast for 15 minutes.

Take the tray from the oven and give everything a good stir. Roast for 15 more minutes, or until the butternut is tender. Remove from the oven and allow to cool.

Once cooled, remove the garlic from its papery skin and add it to the bowl of a food processor. Tip in the butternut, add the lemon juice and blend until smooth. Taste and season with salt and pepper, then serve with a sprinkle of toasted hazelnuts on top.

Freezer adaptation:

If you don't have any frozen butternut squash, try the spiced dip with frozen carrot instead. You could also stir soft crumbly goat's cheese into the butternut dip, if you like.

Will it re-freeze?

The butternut dip will freeze well, if you want to cook a double batch while you have the oven on for roasting the squash. The pea dip is best made fresh.

Serves 4
–
Prep 10 mins
–
Cook 30 mins

THAI BUTTERNUT & COCONUT SOUP

VE

This is a quick and super-simple soup that can be ready in minutes. The combination of sweet butternut and rich coconut milk makes it feel really satisfying. Pay a little more for a premium curry paste; it's the basis of the flavour and you will really taste the difference.

2 tbsp coconut or vegetable oil
200g (7oz) frozen chopped onion
   (or 1 onion, diced)
1 tbsp frozen chopped garlic (or 2 fresh
   cloves, finely chopped)
1 tbsp frozen (or fresh) chopped ginger
2–3 tbsp Thai red curry paste
   (depending on the paste)
750g (1lb 10oz) frozen butternut
   squash cubes
500ml (17fl oz/2 cups) vegetable stock
1 × 400g (14oz) can coconut milk
sea salt and ground black pepper
a handful of Thai basil or a sprinkling
   of coriander (cilantro), to serve
   (optional)

Heat the oil in a large saucepan over a low–medium heat and add the diced onion, garlic and ginger. Allow to cook for a good 5–10 minutes or until really soft. Turn the heat up to medium–high, add the curry paste and mix into the onions for a couple of minutes. Add the butternut squash and the stock, pop a lid on the pan and bring the liquid to a boil. Leave to simmer for 20 minutes or so until the butternut cubes are tender.

Once the butternut is cooked through, reduce the heat to low–medium, add the coconut milk to the pan and stir in. Heat gently, then turn off the heat. Blitz using a stick blender or transfer to a liquidizer and blend until smooth. Taste and season with salt and pepper

Serve with Thai basil leaves or coriander sprinkled over the top, if you have them.

Will it re-freeze?

Absolutely – this is a great one for freezing. Allow to defrost naturally or in the microwave and reheat in a saucepan or in the microwave.

Serves 4
–
Prep 10 mins
–
Cook 35 mins

Veg

SWEETCORN & PEPPER HUSHPUPPIES v

Studded with frozen sweetcorn and peppers, the cornmeal gives these fritters a golden crispness that makes them ridiculously moreish. They are like tasty little lumps of fried cornbread and make a brilliant dipper for a crowd. I like to serve them with a smoky barbecue sauce for dunking, as a nod to their southern USA origins.

100g (3½oz) frozen sweetcorn
100g (3½oz) frozen sliced mixed (bell) peppers
200g (7oz) ground instant polenta (cornmeal)
4 tbsp plain (all-purpose) flour
2 tsp sea salt flakes (or 1 tsp fine salt), plus extra for sprinkling
1 tsp caster (superfine) sugar
1½ tsp baking powder
2 large eggs, lightly beaten
225ml (8fl oz/scant 1 cup) milk
6 spring onions (scallions), finely sliced, plus optional extra to sprinkle
sunflower or vegetable oil, for deep frying
barbecue sauce, to serve

Allow the sweetcorn and peppers to defrost in a sieve (strainer), so that any water can drain away and they dry out a little.

Put the polenta, flour, salt, sugar and baking powder in a large mixing bowl. Add the eggs and 150ml (5fl oz/scant ⅔ cup) of the milk and mix until you have a thick batter. Stir in the sweetcorn, peppers and spring onions and leave to rest for 20 minutes.

Meanwhile, fill a small saucepan one-third full of oil (or use a deep-fat fryer) and heat over a medium heat until a small ball of the batter dropped into the oil sizzles on contact.

Just before you cook the hushpuppies, mix in the remaining milk to slacken the batter. Using 2 teaspoons, scoop walnut-sized balls of the batter, and drop them into the oil. Add a few at a time to the pan, being careful not to overcrowd it. Cook the hushpuppies for about 4 minutes, turning occasionally, until they are golden brown all over. The middles should still be soft, but not doughy and uncooked. Remove them from the oil with a slotted spoon and drain on a plate lined with kitchen paper while you repeat to cook the rest of the batter.

Serve the hushpuppies hot, sprinkled with salt flakes and spring onions, if you like, and with barbecue sauce for dipping.

Will it re-freeze?

Yes, you can freeze these and then reheat on a baking tray in the oven for 15 minutes or so until piping hot throughout.

Serves 4
–
Prep 20 mins
–
Cook 20 mins

Veg

GREEN PANCAKES WITH INDIAN SPICED LEEKS & CHICKPEAS v

This makes a great light lunch for four, but if you want to bulk it up a little, fry off some paneer until golden and stir it into the leek mixture at the end. The pancakes are a little more delicate than usual because of the spinach in them, so make sure you have a good non-stick pan at the ready.

1 tsp cumin seeds
1 tsp coriander seeds
1 tsp mustard seeds
15g (½oz/1 tbsp) butter
1 tbsp olive oil
200g (7oz) frozen chopped onion (or 1 onion, diced)
1 tbsp frozen chopped garlic (or 2 fresh cloves, finely chopped)
1 tbsp frozen (or fresh) chopped ginger
1 green chilli, deseeded and finely chopped
600g (1lb 5oz) frozen sliced leeks
1 × 400g (14oz) can chickpeas, drained and rinsed
2 tsp garam masala
150g (5½oz) crème fraîche
2 tbsp lemon juice
sea salt and ground black pepper

For the pancakes
120g (4¼oz) frozen spinach
140g (5oz/heaped 1 cup) plain (all-purpose) flour
300ml (10½fl oz/1¼ cups) milk
3 large eggs
2 tbsp frozen chopped coriander (cilantro)
butter or oil, for greasing

To serve (optional)
fresh coriander (cilantro) sprigs
crispy fried onions
lemon wedges

Will it re-freeze?
The leek filling will re-freeze, but you'll need to make the pancakes fresh for best results.

First make the pancake batter, so it can rest for a little while. Put the frozen spinach chunks in a food processor and blitz to break them down. Add all the remaining the ingredients (except the fat for greasing) and season well with salt and pepper, then blitz until combined. Set aside until needed. Preheat the oven to a very low heat.

For the leek filling, heat a large sauté pan over medium heat, add the spice seeds and cook for a couple of minutes until smelling toasty. Add the butter, oil and onion to the pan and continue to cook for another 8 minutes or so until the onion is softened and beginning to pick up some colour. Add the garlic, ginger, chilli and the leeks and pop a lid on the pan. Cook for 5–8 minutes with the lid on until the leeks have defrosted. Remove the lid, turn the heat up to high, and cook for another 8–10 minutes until all the liquid has mostly evaporated and the leeks are tender. Add the chickpeas, garam masala, crème fraîche and lemon juice to the pan and stir everything together. Taste and season with salt and black pepper. Set aside while you cook the pancakes.

Grease a non-stick frying pan and place over a medium heat. Once hot, pour in a ladleful of the batter and swirl it around until it coats the base of the pan. Leave to cook for a couple of minutes until the mixture has set and you can move it around by shaking the pan. Flip the pancake carefully using a spatula and cook for another 30 seconds or so on the other side. Tip the pancake out onto a plate and keep warm in the oven, then repeat to make four large pancakes in total.

Briefly rewarm the filling if necessary, then serve the pancakes filled with the creamy leek mixture and sprinkled with coriander and crispy onions, and with lemon wedges on the side for squeezing, if you like.

Serves 4
–
Prep 20 mins
–
Cook 40 mins

WARM ROASTED MAPLE SPROUT, PEARL BARLEY & HAZELNUT SALAD VE

Freezing doesn't help the already much-maligned sprout, but I was determined to redeem them. The key to this is to not let them get any more waterlogged than they probably already will be after their time in the freezer. Get them out of the freezer a few hours in advance and leave them to defrost naturally on a plate lined with kitchen paper to absorb any water.

150g (5½oz) pearl barley
350g (12oz) small round shallots, peeled and halved if large
2 tbsp olive oil
75g (2½oz) blanched hazelnuts
600g (1lb 5oz) frozen button (small) Brussels sprouts
3 tbsp maple syrup
a large handful of parsley, roughly chopped
sea salt and ground black pepper

For the dressing
2 tbsp maple syrup
2 tbsp olive oil
finely grated zest of ½ orange
2 tbsp freshly squeezed orange juice
1 tbsp sherry vinegar (vegan, if necessary)

Put the barley in a saucepan of water and bring to the boil. Once boiling, turn the heat down to a simmer and cook for about 25 minutes, or until just cooked. Drain and leave to steam dry and cool in the colander.

Preheat the oven to 200°C/400°F/gas mark 6.

Put the shallots in a roasting pan and drizzle over the olive oil. Pop in the hot oven for 10 minutes to start them off.

Put the hazelnuts on a small baking tray and pop them in the oven on the shelf below the shallots.

After 10 minutes, remove both baking trays from the oven. Set the hazelnuts aside to cool and add the Brussels to the pan with the shallots. Drizzle over the maple syrup and stir so everything is well coated. Return the pan to the oven for a further 10 minutes.

Meanwhile, roughly chop the hazelnuts. Mix together all the ingredients for the dressing and season well with salt and pepper. Set these aside.

Add the barley to the roasting pan and return to the oven for a further 10–15 minutes, until the barley is starting to brown and crisp and the brussels are really starting to take on some colour.

Pour the dressing all over the pan and toss to coat everything. Add most of the hazelnuts and parsley and stir in. Taste and season with more salt and pepper, if it needs it.

Transfer to a serving bowl and serve warm, sprinkled with the remaining hazelnuts and parsley.

Freezer adaptation:
If you happen to have any smoked bacon lardons in the freezer, a few of these fried to crisp up and sprinkled over the top is lovely.

Will it re-freeze?
Brussels that have been frozen and defrosted twice are beyond redemption. Eat this one fresh out of the oven.

Serves 4
–
Prep 15 mins
–
Cook 50 mins

MIXED PEPPER, THYME & CHEDDAR TART v

This tasty tart makes a lovely lunch for four with a salad or is perfect for a picnic. Along with frozen peppers and sheets of pastry, thyme is one of those freezer essentials (hardy herbs freeze really well, see page 9) which can be brought out to add a lovely scent to a simple tart such as this.

500g (1lb 2oz) frozen mixed sliced peppers
plain (all-purpose) flour, for dusting
1 × 375g (13oz) sheet of frozen ready-rolled shortcrust pastry, defrosted
2 tbsp olive oil
1 red onion, finely sliced
1 tbsp frozen chopped garlic (or 2 fresh cloves, finely chopped)
leaves from 2 bushy sprigs of thyme
175g (6oz) crème fraîche
3 large egg yolks
140g (5oz) Cheddar cheese, grated
sea salt and ground black pepper

Tip the frozen peppers into a colander and run warm water over them to defrost. Leave them to strain and dry in the colander for a good hour.

On a lightly floured surface, roll out the pastry a little more lengthways to make it long enough to fit the tin, then use it to line a 36 × 13cm (14 × 5in) tart tin. Pierce the pastry base several times with a fork and place in the fridge to chill for 30 minutes. Preheat the oven to 190°C/375°F/gas mark 5.

While the pastry is chilling, make the filling. Heat the olive oil in a frying pan and add the onion. Sauté gently for a good 8 minutes until starting to soften and turn translucent. Add the garlic and thyme leaves and cook for another few minutes, then add the peppers and stir until everything is well combined. Season well with salt and pepper.

Line the pastry case with baking parchment and fill with baking beans, then blind bake for 12 minutes. Remove the parchment and baking beans and return to the oven for another 5 minutes until the base is beginning to dry out and turn golden.

Mix together the crème fraîche, egg yolks and about 100g (3½oz) of the cheese, reserving the rest to sprinkle over the top. Season the mixture with salt and pepper.

Spoon the creamy filling into the pastry case, spreading the cheese evenly, then top with the pepper mixture, again spreading it evenly over the top. Finish by sprinkling over the reserved grated Cheddar. Bake for about 25 minutes, or until the top is golden, the filling is set and the pastry is cooked through and golden. Serve warm.

Will it re-freeze?

Yes. Let it defrost, then warm it in a low–medium oven for about 10 minutes to crisp-up the pastry.

Serves 4
–
Prep 20 mins
–
Cook 50 mins

HONEYED CARROT & ROSEMARY TARTE TATIN v

This looks (and tastes) far more fancy than its few humble ingredients might suggest. If you can't find frozen Chantenay carrots, just use the same weight of frozen slices and blanch for just a few seconds to defrost, then follow the recipe as below. It works just as well, especially if you take the time to arrange the slices in pretty circles.

350g (12oz) frozen Chantenay carrots
50g (1¾oz/3½ tbsp) butter
1 tbsp oil
2 tbsp clear runny honey
a few small sprigs of frozen (or fresh)
    rosemary
a sheet of frozen ready-rolled puff
    pastry (or about 250g/9oz from
    a block), defrosted
sea salt and ground black pepper

Will it re-freeze?

You can freeze this once cooked. Just let it defrost naturally, then reheat gently in the oven to crisp up the pastry and warm the carrots through. You may want to brush the top with a little melted butter to make it glossy again.

Blanch the carrots in hot water for 2 minutes until just defrosted. Leave to drain and steam dry in a colander.

Preheat the oven to 200°C/400°F/gas mark 6 and find yourself a heavy-based ovenproof 20cm (8in) frying pan (such as a small skillet).

Put the butter and oil in the pan and heat on the hob until the butter is melted, then stir in the honey until melted and well incorporated.

Put the dry carrots in a bowl and pour the contents of the pan over them. Toss so that they are all coated evenly in the buttery mixture. Season well with salt and pepper.

Lay the rosemary sprigs over the bottom of the pan – be careful as it will still be hot for a while if it's a heavy pan. Arrange the carrots over the base of the pan, making a pretty circular pattern with them (they are perfectly shaped for this, if their tips are arranged pointing inwards). Pour any of the butter left in the bowl over the carrots in the pan. Place the pan in the oven and cook for 10 minutes so the carrots can start to cook and caramelize.

Cut out a 20cm (8in) diameter circle from the pastry sheet and pop it in the fridge to keep cool.

Once the first 10 minutes are up, remove the pan from the oven and lay the pastry circle over the top of the carrots, tucking it in around the sides. Pierce the pastry with a knife so that the steam can escape, and return the pan to the oven for 45 minutes until the pastry is puffed and golden.

Carefully (the pan will be volcanically hot) place a plate on top of the pan and, wearing oven gloves, invert the pan so that the tart tips out onto the plate. Serve, but don't expect people to eat the rosemary sprigs! They are for decoration at this point and will already have imparted their flavour into the carrots.

Serves 4
–
Prep 15 mins
–
Cook 1 hour

MIXED FLORET GRATIN v

This flexible veggie and cheese bake can be made up with whatever florets you have to hand – broccoli, cauliflower or a mixture. Just aim for about 700g (1lb 9oz) in total.

350g (12oz) frozen broccoli florets
350g (12oz) frozen cauliflower florets
40g (1½oz/3 tbsp) butter
30g (1oz/4 tbsp) plain (all-purpose) flour
350ml (12fl oz/1½ cups) whole milk
120g (4¼oz) mature Cheddar cheese
a grating of nutmeg
30g (1oz) frozen (or fresh) breadcrumbs
sea salt and ground black pepper

Will it re-freeze?

It's best not to do the final bake on this one. If you want some for freezing, double the recipe (or just freeze half) and assemble in a foil tray. That way, you can just pull it out the freezer and bake it off from frozen whenever a comforting cheesy bake is required. Bake at 180°C/350°F/gas mark 4 for 30–40 minutes, covering the top with a piece of foil if it looks as if it's browning too quickly.

Preheat the oven to 200°C/400°F/gas mark 6 and get a large pan of water boiling.

Blanch the broccoli and cauliflower florets in the boiling water for 1 minute only, until defrosted and just beginning to soften. Leave to cool and steam dry in the colander.

Meanwhile, make the cheese sauce. Melt the butter in a large saucepan, then add the flour and mix in with a whisk. Cook for a couple of minutes until the flavour of the flour is beginning to cook out, then start adding the milk, a splash at a time, whisking in between additions to get rid of any lumps as you go. Once all the milk is added, cook for a few minutes more until the sauce has thickened, remembering it will cook a little more in the gratin, so keep it slightly runnier than you would a standard white sauce. Add all but a small handful of the cheese, then taste and season with a grating of nutmeg and salt and pepper.

Add the broccoli and cauliflower florets to the pan of sauce, stir until they are well coated, then tip the lot into a baking dish that will fit everything comfortably. Sprinkle the reserved cheese over the top, then finish with an even sprinkling of the frozen (or fresh) breadcrumbs. Bake for 20–25 minutes, until the top is crispy and light golden and it's rewarmed throughout.

Serves 4
–
Prep 10 mins
–
Cook 40 mins

Veg

MUSHROOM & RED WINE TAGLIATELLE v

You can now get some lovely assortments of frozen mixed mushrooms – not just simple sliced cup mushrooms but mixes with more exotic varieties and better flavour. This is quite rich, so you don't need too much of the sauce. Just toss it through the pasta and top with a good sprinkling of Parmesan, then serve with a fresh and peppery rocket salad on the side to cut through the richness.

2 tbsp olive oil
40g (1½oz/3 tbsp) salted butter
200g (7oz) frozen chopped onion
    (or 1 onion, diced)
1½ tbsp frozen chopped garlic (or
    3 fresh cloves, finely chopped)
leaves from 2 bushy sprigs of frozen
    (or fresh) thyme, plus extra sprigs
    to serve
600g (1lb 5oz) frozen mixed
    mushrooms
180ml (6fl oz/¾ cup) red wine (a mini
    bottle or frozen in cubes, see
    page 10)
1 vegetable jelly stock pot
sea salt and ground black pepper
freshly cooked tagliatelle, to serve
shaved Parmesan, to serve

Heat the oil and butter together in a large saucepan and add the onion. Cook for about 6 minutes until it is softening and turning translucent. Add the garlic and the thyme leaves and cook for another 3 minutes.

Add the frozen mushrooms and cook until they are defrosted and wilted down and a lot of the liquid has evaporated. Add the red wine and the stock pot to the pan and cook until the liquid has reduced by half. Taste and season well with salt and pepper.

Serve the mushroom and red wine ragù stirred through freshly cooked tagliatelle, sprinkled with Parmesan shavings.

Freezer adaptation:

If you can't find a bag of one of the more exotic collections, simple frozen sliced mushrooms will still work, of course, but just may not feel as fancy.

Will it re-freeze?

Yes, the sauce will happily keep in the freezer and can be defrosted and used straight from the microwave.

Serves 4
–
Prep 15 mins
–
Cook 30 mins

Veg

GREEN BEAN & HALLOUMI MASALA v

This quick curry, which makes the most of a bag of vibrant green beans, is a great weeknight dinner. option. It can be easily made vegan by switching out the halloumi for tofu and using a plant-based yogurt or cream. Serve with rice or naan breads.

2 tbsp olive oil, plus a drizzle for the halloumi
200g (7oz) frozen chopped onion (or 1 onion, diced)
1 tbsp frozen chopped garlic (or 2 fresh cloves, finely chopped)
1½ tbsp frozen (or fresh) chopped ginger
1 tsp ground cumin
1 tsp ground coriander
1 tsp ground turmeric
1 tsp paprika
2 tsp garam masala
1 × 400g (14oz) can chopped tomatoes
1 tbsp tomato purée (paste)
1 tsp soft brown sugar
250g (9oz) frozen green beans, snapped in half
1 × 225g (8oz) pack halloumi, cut into 1.5cm (⅝in) cubes
100g (3½oz) thick Greek yogurt
sea salt and ground black pepper
30g (1oz) flaked almonds, toasted, to serve

Heat the oil in a large sauté pan over a low–medium heat and fry the onion with a pinch of salt for 5 minutes until softening. Add the garlic, ginger and spices and fry for another few minutes until everything is smelling aromatic and the onions are completely tender. Add the tomatoes, tomato purée, sugar and 60ml (2fl oz/¼ cup) water, pop a lid on the pan and simmer for 5 minutes, stirring occasionally to stop it catching.

Add the frozen green beans to the pan, pop the lid back on and simmer for another 5 minutes, until the beans are cooked and tender.

Meanwhile, in a large non-stick frying pan, heat a drizzle of oil. Pat the cubes of halloumi dry with a piece of kitchen paper to remove as much excess water as you can and add them to the frying pan. Fry over a medium–high heat, watching closely and turning the cubes regularly until they are golden brown on all sides.

Stir the yogurt into the curry until well combined, then add the fried halloumi. Taste and season with salt and pepper.

Serve the curry sprinkled with toasted almond flakes.

Freezer adaptation:

If you don't have green beans, you could substitute the same weight of frozen peas or even edamame beans.

Will it re-freeze?

Yes, this is a good one for batch cooking. The halloumi will never be quite as soft and yielding as it is when you eat it hot and fresh, but it will soften and be fine in a curry. Divide into individual tubs, and just bring out the number of portions you need. Defrost and reheat in the microwave while you're cooking up some fresh rice or warming naan in the oven.

Serves 4
–
Prep 15 mins
–
Cook 20 mins

FREEZER FEAST: GREEN RISOTTO v

The joy of this is that you can use pretty much everything in your freezer that happens to be green: peas, beans, broccoli, edamame and, of course, freezer-staple pesto (see page 11) for a serious flavour boost. Adapt it to whatever you have to hand. If you are vegetarian, make sure you go for a Parmesan-style cheese that is suitable – in both the risotto and the pesto.

30g (1oz/2 tbsp) butter
1 tbsp olive oil
200g (7oz) frozen chopped onion (or 1 onion, diced)
1½ tbsp frozen chopped garlic (or 3 fresh cloves, finely chopped)
250g (9oz) arborio risotto rice
180ml (6fl oz/¾ cup) white wine (a mini bottle or frozen in cubes, see page 10)
700ml (24fl oz/3 cups) hot vegetable or chicken stock
400g (14oz) small green freezer veg (peas, beans, edamame, broad/fava beans, etc.)
40g (1½oz) grated Parmesan, plus extra to serve (vegetarian, if necessary)
4–5 tbsp Pesto Genovese (see page 11)
sea salt and ground black pepper

Melt the butter with the olive oil in a large saucepan over a low–medium heat. Add the onion and cook for a good 8–10 minutes until really soft and translucent. Add the garlic and cook for a couple more minutes.

Add the rice to the pan and stir around for a minute or so to coat the grains in the oil, then add the wine. Cook for 4–5 minutes, stirring regularly, until most of the liquid has cooked off, then begin adding the hot stock. Add it a ladleful at a time, only adding more when the previous addition has been absorbed by the rice.

When you have added almost all of the stock and the rice is almost cooked, add your frozen veg to the pan along with the remaining stock. Cook for about 5 minutes more, until the rice is tender with just a little bite and the veg is just cooked. Stir in the Parmesan and let it melt into the mixture, then stir in the pesto and season to taste with salt and pepper. Serve with extra Parmesan for sprinkling.

Will it re-freeze?

Yes, although you will lose your al dente bite on the rice, but it will still be tasty. Simply leave to thaw naturally or pop in the microwave, and reheat either in the microwave or in a saucepan.

Serves 4
–
Prep 15 mins
–
Cook 30 mins

Veg

MUSHROOM & PEPPER STROGANOFF WITH GNOCCHI v

This is creamy, smoky, sweet, simple to cook and oh-so delicious. And if that wasn't enough, it freezes really well and so can be frozen in appropriately sized portions for your household and just popped in the microwave whenever you need a quick and comforting supper. I love it teamed with gnocchi that's been fried until crisped and golden, but you could also serve it with rice or pasta ribbons.

1 tbsp olive oil
1 tbsp butter
200g (7oz) frozen chopped onion (or 1 onion, diced)
½ tbsp frozen chopped garlic (or 1 fresh clove, finely chopped)
1 tbsp sweet smoked paprika
600g (1lb 5oz) frozen mixed mushrooms
500g (1lb 2oz) sliced frozen peppers
1 vegetable jelly stock pot
2 tsp Dijon mustard
120g (4oz) crème fraîche
a small bunch of parsley, chopped, or a handful of frozen chopped parsley
sea salt and ground black pepper
gnocchi, to serve

Add the oil and butter to a large frying or sauté pan. Add the onion and sauté for 5 minutes until really starting to soften. Add the garlic and the sweet smoked paprika and stir in, then add the frozen mushrooms and cook for about 5 minutes until the mushrooms are defrosted and beginning to cook down.

Add the peppers and cook for a couple of minutes longer, then add the stock pot and the mustard. Cook for 15 or so minutes more until everything is well cooked and the liquid has reduced (frozen vegetables will let out quite a lot of water, so be patient and cook this off).

Stir the crème fraîche and most of the parsley into the sauce and season generously with salt and pepper to taste. Serve with gnocchi, sprinkled with the reserved parsley.

Freezer adaptation:

If you happen to have any pork or beef steak in the freezer, you could let the meat defrost then cut it into strips. Fry it quickly over a high heat until caramelized, but still a little pink in the middle (less so, if using pork). Set aside while you cook the stroganoff, then add it back in at the very last minute just to heat through gently.

Will it re-freeze?

Yes; simply leave to thaw naturally or pop in the microwave, and reheat either in the microwave or in a saucepan.

Serves 4
–
Prep 15 mins
–
Cook 30 mins

'PUMPKIN', PECAN & MAPLE PIE v

I've used frozen butternut squash here, as a bag of squash chunks is far more likely to be found in the freezer at mine. But if you happen to have pumpkin instead, feel free to use that.

1kg (2lb 4oz) frozen butternut squash chunks
5 tbsp maple syrup, plus optional extra for brushing
½ tsp ground cinnamon
½ tsp ground ginger
A grating of fresh nutmeg, plus extra for the top
375g (13oz) frozen shortcrust or sweet shortcrust pastry, defrosted
plain (all-purpose) flour, for dusting
1 × 170ml (5½fl oz) can evaporated milk
1 large egg, plus 2 large egg yolks
100g (3½oz) pecan halves
whipped cream or crème fraîche, to serve

Freezer adaptation:

If you can find actual frozen pumpkin, do use that. But this is not very common in UK freezer aisles, thus the use of butternut.

Will it re-freeze?

Yes; just be sure to let it defrost at room temperature first, then rewarm it in the oven at low–medium heat so that the pastry crisps up again.

Preheat the oven to 200°C/400°F/gas mark 6. Spread the squash chunks out on a large baking tray (or use two) and bake for 30 minutes, until mostly cooked. Remove the tray from the oven, drizzle with 2 tbsp of the maple syrup and sprinkle over the spices. Stir well to coat the squash, then return to the oven for a further 20 minutes until it all starts to caramelize. Remove from the oven and leave to cool.

Roll the pastry out on a lightly flour-dusted surface and use it to line a 23cm (9in) diameter pie plate. Cut off the excess leaving a couple of millimetres overhanging the lip of the tin, then crimp around the edge, slightly tucking the pastry under the lip to encourage it not to shrink back. Pierce the bottom of the base a few times with a fork and pop in the fridge to chill for 20 minutes. Preheat the oven to 190°C/375°F/gas mark 5, if it's not already hot from the squash.

While the pastry is chilling, prepare the filling. Put the roasted butternut squash in a food processor with the evaporated milk and the remaining maple syrup and blend until smooth. Separate the whole egg and add the yolk to the food processor with the other two yolks, setting the white aside. Blend again until everything is smooth.

When the pastry has chilled, scrunch up a large piece of baking parchment, then flatten it out again (this makes it more pliable). Use it to line the pastry case, making sure the whole pie plate is covered. Fill with baking beans and blind bake for 15 minutes, then remove the plate from the oven and remove the parchment and beans. Bake for 5 minutes until starting to turn light golden. Lightly beat the reserved egg white, then brush it all over the pastry case – this will help to waterproof it so the pastry doesn't go soggy. Return it to the oven for a final minute to set the egg white.

Turn the oven down to 180°C/350°F/gas mark 4. Tip the filling into the pastry case and smooth level. Arrange the pecan halves in a circle around the top, just inside the pastry edge and grate a little nutmeg over the centre of the pie. Bake for 30–40 minutes, until the filling is set. Allow to cool a little before slicing and serving with cream or crème fraîche.

Serves 6–8
–
Prep 20 mins
–
Cook 1½ hours

FRUIT

Finally to the sweet stuff... With a bag of frozen fruit at your disposal, the joy starts at breakfast (see Cherry Bakewell Porridge), through to snack time (try the Spiced Blackberry Flapjacks) and on to a selection of fruity desserts. From treats for the kids, like Strawberry Jam and Baked Alaska, to some strictly adult creations – try the Warm Dark Fruit Zabaglione Cups or the Berries and Gin – to a Tropical Meringue Feast (pictured here) that's sure to appeal to all.

CHERRY BAKEWELL PORRIDGE VE

This wholesome brekkie is generous on the fruit as it's good to get a daily portion in! The ingredients listed are for one portion, so just scale up as you need to. The key to really creamy porridge (oatmeal) is the slow cooking and continued stirring. I also like to use whole rolled oats rather than porridge oats for a little more texture, but use what you prefer or have to hand.

15g (½oz) flaked almonds
50g (1¾oz) whole rolled oats
150–200ml (5–7fl oz/⅔–scant 1 cup)
   milk (vegan, if necessary)
80g (2¾oz) frozen cherries
½ tsp vanilla extract
a drizzle of maple syrup, to serve
   (optional)

Start by toasting the almonds. Place them in a small, dry frying pan and toast for a few minutes, shaking the pan so they cook evenly, until they are golden brown and smelling toasty. Tip them onto a plate and set aside.

Put the oats in a small saucepan and add 150ml (5fl oz/ scant ⅔ cup) of the milk, the frozen cherries and vanilla extract. Cook over a very low heat, stirring gently, for about 5 minutes, until the oats are cooked and the cherries have defrosted and have begun to break down and turn the porridge a pretty purple. If it starts to look a little dry, add the remaining milk.

Pour the porridge into a bowl. The cherries and vanilla will sweeten the porridge, but if you'd like it a little sweeter, add a drizzle of maple syrup. Sprinkle over the toasted almonds and serve.

Freezer adaptation:
You could try and use any frozen berry you have for this. Feel free to vary the flavouring and nuts to match.

Will it re-freeze?
It doesn't, and you wouldn't need to anyway as it's so quick.

Serves 1
–
Prep 5 mins
–
Cook 8 mins

Fruit

AUTUMN-SPICED BLACKBERRY FLAPJACKS v

My mum's flapjacks were always popular on those primary school birthday occasions when we were required to bring in a baked treat for the class. This is her recipe, embellished with a little spice and some frozen blackberries. Frozen fruit works really well for this – the berries hold their own a bit more in the oven.

170g (6oz) salted butter, plus extra
   for greasing
2 tbsp honey
160g (5¾oz) soft light brown sugar
340g (12oz) porridge oats
2 tsp ground mixed spice
120g (4¼oz) frozen blackberries

Preheat the oven to 180°C/350°F/gas mark 4 and grease a 20 × 25cm (8 × 10in) brownie tin with butter.

Melt the butter in a large saucepan, then stir in the honey and the sugar. Add the oats and the spice and mix well until all the oats are well coated.

Tip the mixture into the prepared baking tin and smooth to roughly level. Scatter the frozen blackberries over the top, spreading them evenly, then push them into the mixture. Smooth everything level again, pressing the mixture down firmly this time – a potato masher is handy for this.

Bake for 20–25 minutes, until golden on top. Allow to cool until almost cold in the tin, then tip out onto a board. Slice into 12 squares and serve.

Freezer adaptation:

Feel free to try this with the same weight of frozen raspberries instead, or frozen blackcurrants.

Will it re-freeze?

I highly doubt you will have the occasion or opportunity to try freezing these. But they will keep for a few days in the fridge (to keep the blackberries fresh).

Makes 12
–
Prep 10 mins
–
Cook 25 mins

Fruit

PEACH MELBA BUTTERED BETTY v

For anyone not familiar with a 'betty', it's an American dessert that's like a crumble, but made with buttery breadcrumbs instead of the usual flour and butter mix. Using freezer fruit and frozen crumbs, you can make this homely pudding even if you have barely anything in the fridge – except of course the good salted butter that gives this its wonderfully rich flavour.

170g (6oz) fresh or frozen breadcrumbs (from about 4 thick-cut slices of bread)
90g (3¼oz) good salted butter
40g (1½oz) soft light brown sugar
500g (1lb 2oz) frozen peach and/or nectarine slices, defrosted
150g (5½oz) frozen raspberries, defrosted
custard, crème fraîche or ice cream, to serve

Preheat the oven to 180°C/350°F/gas mark 4.

Spread the crumbs out on two large baking trays and bake for 3 minutes. Take the trays out, stir the crumbs, then return them to the oven for another 2 minutes until they are all dried out and light golden. Tip the crumbs into a large bowl. Leave the oven on.

Melt the butter and sugar together in a saucepan, then pour it over the crumbs. Mix the butter into the crumbs well so they are all evenly coated. Getting your hands in and massaging everything helps here and makes it much easier to distribute the butter than with a spoon. Set aside.

Spread half of the peaches over the base of a baking dish and scatter half of the raspberries over the top. Sprinkle half of the breadcrumbs over the fruit, then repeat the layers again to use up the rest of the fruit and crumbs.

Place the dish in the oven and bake for 20 minutes, or until the fruit is piping hot and the crumbs are a richer golden colour. Serve immediately with custard, crème fraîche or ice cream

Freezer adaptation:
Peaches and raspberries are a classic combination, but there's no need to restrict yourself to this – feel free to experiment with whatever fruit you have.

Will it re-freeze?
You can re-freeze this in foil containers, then defrost and reheat gently in the oven. Cover with a piece of foil if it is browning too much.

Serves 4–6
–
Prep 10 mins
–
Cook 30 mins

Fruit

RHUBARB, STRAWBERRY & ELDERFLOWER FOOL v

The rhubarb that you can buy frozen in bags doesn't tend to be the beautifully pink forced rhubarb that can be easily used to adorn tarts. It tends to be the mostly greenish stuff which cooks down to a rather sludgy and unappealing brown, but still tastes delicious. Adding a few strawberries will up the pink and the floral, aromatic flavours work well together and with that of the elderflower.

350g (12oz) frozen rhubarb slices
150g (5½oz) frozen strawberries, plus extra to decorate
90ml (3fl oz/6 tbsp) elderflower cordial
200ml (7fl oz/scant 1 cup) double (heavy) cream
1 tbsp icing (confectioner's) sugar
150g (5½oz) Greek yogurt
fresh elderflowers (or other edible flowers), to decorate, if available
shortbread biscuits, to serve (optional)

Put the frozen rhubarb and strawberries into a large saucepan. Pop a lid on the pan and cook over low–medium heat for 15–20 minutes, stirring regularly, until the rhubarb is tender and cooked down, but not a mush (the strawberries will probably cook right down as they don't need as much cooking, which is perfect – we want the colour from their juice).

Once the rhubarb is cooked, turn off the heat and pour in the elderflower cordial. Stir everything together and allow to cool.

Put the double cream and icing sugar in a mixing bowl and whisk to soft peaks. Fold in the Greek yogurt until all combined, then roughly fold in the cooled fruit purée, leaving large streaks in the mixture so you have a marbled effect. Divide it between four dessert bowls and place in the fridge to chill until ready to serve.

Decorate the top of the fools with some fresh elderflowers, or other edible flowers, if available, and serve with shortbread biscuits.

Freezer adaptation:
Make the purée out of any freezer fruit you have, then stir into yogurt and cream as per the recipe for fools of all varieties.

Will it re-freeze?
Technically yes, but the texture won't be as smooth and creamy, so best to eat it fresh.

Serves 6
–
Prep 15 mins
–
Cook 20 mins

CHAI-SPICED PEACH RICE PUDDING BRÛLÉE v

For a comforting, wintry, rib-sticking sort of dessert, this one is hard to beat. Homely rice pudding is perked up with Indian spices and sweet juicy peaches, and all finished with a layer of crisp, caramelized sugar.

160g (5¾oz) pudding rice
4 star anise
5 cloves
8 cardamom pods, bashed
30g (1oz/2 tbsp) butter
a good grating of nutmeg
1 tsp ground ginger
1 tsp ground cinnamon
a pinch of salt
a grind of black pepper
500–600ml (17–21fl oz/2–2½ cups) whole milk, plus extra if needed
1 × 397g (14oz) can condensed milk
300g (10½oz) frozen sliced peaches and/or nectarines
caster (superfine) sugar, to sprinkle

Preheat the oven to 140°C/275°F/gas mark 1.

Put the rice in a large frying pan and toast over a medium heat for a couple of minutes. Add the star anise, cloves and cardamom pods and toast for a couple more minutes until everything is smelling aromatic. Add the butter and let it melt, stirring to coat the rice, then grate in some nutmeg, and add the ground spices, salt and pepper. Stir until everything is well incorporated, then add 500ml (17fl oz/ 2 cups) of the whole milk and the condensed milk and mix to combine. Continue to cook for a couple of minutes until the liquid is hot, then carefully pour everything into a large casserole dish and cover with a lid or a piece of foil. Transfer the dish to the preheated oven and cook for 2 hours, stirring every half an hour or so.

After 2 hours, remove the pan from the oven and add the peaches. If it's looking a little dry, add a splash more milk. Give everything a good stir and return to the oven for 30 minutes, covered again. By this point the rice should be tender and the peaches cooked. Switch the cooker to the grill (broiler) setting on high (or you can use a blow torch for this, in which case just turn the oven off).

Sprinkle a layer of sugar over the top of the pudding and caramelize it, either under the hot grill or with a blow torch. Serve immediately.

Will it re-freeze?

Yes; simply leave to thaw naturally or pop in the microwave, and reheat either in the microwave or in a saucepan. Give it a good stir to bring it back together – you will lose the crisp coating, but it will still taste delicious.

Serves 6
–
Prep 10 mins
–
Cook 2½ hours

Fruit

FREEZER FEAST: TROPICAL MERINGUE GÂTEAU v

Frozen tropical fruits are brilliant for delivering a hit of sunshine all year round, and mean this crowd-pleasing dessert can be whipped up from just a few basic freezer and pantry ingredients. You will need to think ahead, as it's easiest to make the meringue the night before and leave it to cool in the oven overnight – but that's a pretty small effort for such a deceptively grand pud!

For the meringue
5 large egg whites
250g (9oz/1¼ cups) caster (superfine) sugar

For the filling and topping
2 × 400g (14oz) cans coconut milk, chilled
1 tbsp icing (confectioner's) sugar (or more, to taste)
500g (1lb 2oz) frozen mango chunks
500g (1lb 2oz) frozen pineapple chunks
20g (⅔oz) coconut flakes, toasted

Preheat the oven to 110°C/225°F/gas mark ½ and line three baking trays with baking parchment. On each sheet of parchment draw a 20cm (8in) round circle, then turn the sheets over so that the pencil doesn't transfer on to the meringue.

Put the egg whites in a clean, grease-free bowl and whisk until frothy. With the mixer running, start adding the sugar, a spoonful at a time, until it has all been incorporated. Whisk the meringue for about 8 minutes longer, or until very stiff and glossy. Spoon the meringue onto the prepared baking sheets, using the circles you have drawn as a guide. Bake for 1 hour, then turn off the heat and let the meringue slowly cool in the cooling oven.

Open the cans of coconut milk and scoop out the solids on top into a mixing bowl. You may need to break them up a bit with the spoon as you go. Beat them until they are smooth, adding a splash of the coconut water from the cans, if needed, to get a thick, smooth cream. Add the icing sugar and whisk in.

To assemble, place a meringue disc on a cake stand or serving plate and top with one third of the coconut cream. Spoon over about a quarter of the fruit and pop the second disc on top. Repeat with the second layer, then pop the final disc on top. Spread the remaining coconut cream over the top of the gâteau and add the remaining fruit, piling it up a little in the centre to create a slight mound.

Finally, sprinkle the top of the gâteau with toasted coconut flakes and serve immediately.

Freezer adaptation:
You could do something similar to this with any bags of fruit you happen to have in the freezer. Berries would also be nice with coconut cream, or you could use whipped cream with a swirl of lemon curd.

Will it re-freeze?
This is definitely one for enjoying fresh.

Serves 8
–
Prep 20 mins
–
Cook 2 hours

MINI LEMON & SUMMER BERRY CHEESECAKES v

Bags of frozen summer berries often contain a high proportion of red- and blackcurrants, which can really be a bit sharp to be truly enjoyable. But team them with this gloriously rich cheesecake and, far from pushing them to the side of the plate, their tanginess provides a welcome tartness next to the decadently creamy filling.

85g (3oz/⅓ cup) unsalted butter, plus extra for greasing
175g (6oz) digestive biscuits (graham crackers)
2 sheets gelatine (or vegetarian alternative)
250g (9oz) crème fraîche
250g (9oz) mascarpone
2 tbsp icing (confectioner's) sugar
2 tbsp freshly squeezed lemon juice
3 tbsp lemon curd
250g (9oz) mixed frozen summer berries, defrosted

Grease a 12-hole loose-based mould or baking tin with butter.

Start by making the bases. Put the butter in a large saucepan over a low heat and melt gently. Meanwhile, pop the biscuits in a sturdy bag and bash with a rolling pin until you have crumbs (or blitz in a food processor). Tip the crumbs into the melted butter and stir everything together. Divide the mixture between the holes of your mould and press down firmly, then put in the fridge to set.

Put the gelatine sheets in a bowl of cold water to soak.

Meanwhile, combine the crème fraîche, mascarpone and icing sugar and beat together well.

Put the lemon juice in a small saucepan and heat gently. Squeeze out the gelatine sheets and add them to the warm juice, then remove from the heat and stir until they are dissolved. Add the gelatine liquid to the cheesecake mix and beat in.

Remove the cheesecake bases from the fridge. Add the lemon curd to the cheesecake mix, but don't stir in fully – you want some marbling in the mix, so just gently swirl in. Divide the mixture between the moulds and smooth the tops, then return to the fridge to set and chill for at least 2 hours.

To serve, remove the cheesecakes from the moulds and spoon the fruit over the tops.

Freezer adaptation:
The opportunities are pretty endless here. You can flavour the cheesecake mix with any curd or flavouring extract you fancy. As for the topping... what other bags of fruit do you have in the freezer?

Will it re-freeze?
Yes, and you can actually serve these as a semi-freddo by letting them just defrost halfway when thawing.

Makes 12
–
Prep 2½ hours
–
Cook 5 mins

MAYAN CHOCOLATE AVOCADO MOUSSE v

The avocado here gives a creamy texture to this indulgent mousse, with a hint of orange and spice. It can be tricky to find star anise ground, but if you have a spice grinder and a few stars, it is worth adding as it really adds another depth to the flavour. You don't have to have the chocolate sauce in the freezer – you can easily cook it off quickly and allow it to cool, then proceed as in the recipe.

1 recipe quantity (about 200g/7oz) Freezer Chocolate Sauce (see page 11), defrosted
100g (3½oz) frozen avocado, defrosted
finely grated zest of 1 orange
freshly squeezed juice from ½ orange
¾ tsp ground cinnamon
½ tsp ground star anise (optional)
a good pinch of chilli powder
3 large egg whites
30g (1oz/3 tbsp) caster (superfine) sugar
20g (⅔oz) dark chocolate, grated, to serve

In a food processor, blend together the chocolate sauce and avocado. Add most of the orange zest (reserving a little for decoration), the orange juice, cinnamon, ground star anise (if using) and chilli powder and blend again to incorporate. Taste and add a little more chilli powder if you'd like a bit more of a tingle, but it shouldn't be hot and spicy – just a hint. Once the mixture is smooth, transfer it to a large mixing bowl.

Put the egg whites in the bowl of a stand mixer and whisk to soft peaks. With the mixer still running, start to add the sugar a little at a time. Once all the sugar is incorporated, keep whisking until a little of the meringue rubbed between your finger and thumb feels smooth and you can't feel any grains of sugar.

Add a large spoonful of the beaten egg whites to the chocolate and avocado and beat in vigorously to slacken the mixture. Then add the rest of the egg whites and fold in gently, being careful not to knock too much air out of the mixture. Once everything is well incorporated and no streaks remain, divide the mousse evenly between six small serving bowls. Chill in the fridge for at least an hour, but you can leave them in there until ready to serve.

To serve, top the mousse with a little grated chocolate and a sprinkling of the reserved orange zest.

Will it re-freeze?

No, as the chocolate sauce has already been frozen. Enjoy this one the day you make it.

Serves 6
–
Prep 1½ hours

Fruit

COCONUT, CHERRY & WHITE CHOCOLATE ICE CREAM VE

Coconut ice cream is one of the easiest to make and is delicious, but the quality of coconut milk you use really does make a difference. My favourite brand for this is Suma Organic – it's so creamy that almost three-quarters of the can sets, with just a little water at the bottom. Cheaper ones will not give you the firmness you need for this, and some are a little bitter, so do try and find a good one.

3 × 400g (14oz) cans good-quality coconut milk
3 tbsp icing (confectioner's) sugar
400g (14oz) frozen dark cherries
150g (5½oz) white chocolate, roughly chopped (vegan, if necessary)
toasted coconut (desiccated/dried shredded or flakes), to sprinkle

The night before you'd like to make the ice cream, put the cans of coconut milk in the fridge to chill and separate.

To make the ice cream, scrape the solid milk from the top of the cans into the bowl of a food processor. Add the sugar and blitz shortly until the mixture is smooth. Add most of the frozen cherries and pulse quickly until the mixture is turning pink but there are still lumps of fruit visible. Remove the blade and just stir in most of the chocolate chunks.

Transfer the ice cream to a 1-litre (35fl oz) container and sprinkle the top with the reserved cherries and chocolate. Freeze for an hour or so until just set, but don't let it get too hard. If you want to freeze it for longer, make sure you get it out of the freezer a good time before you wish to serve it so that it can soften.

Serve the ice cream sprinkled with the toasted coconut.

Will it re-freeze?

Yes, just return what you don't use to the freezer, as you would any other tub of ice cream.

Makes 1 litre
—
Prep 1 hour

Fruit

WARM DARK FRUIT ZABAGLIONE CUPS v

Luscious dark fruits, caramelized almond biscuits and creamy, not to mention boozy, zabaglione combine in this very adult dessert. Blackcurrants are sadly one of the lesser-stocked fresh berries in supermarkets, but you can often find them in the freezer section. Or buy them when they are in season and freeze them. If you can't find blackcurrants, see the adaptation below.

120g (4¼oz) amaretti biscuits
200g (7oz) frozen cherries
150g (5½oz) frozen blackcurrants
1–2 tbsp icing (confectioner's) sugar

For the zabaglione
3 large egg yolks
5 tbsp Marsala wine
45g (1½oz/scant ¼ cup) sugar

Break the amaretti biscuits up with your hands and divide them between four glass serving dishes.

Put the cherries, blackcurrants and icing sugar into a small saucepan and cook over a low heat for about 10 minutes, until the fruit is just starting to break down and you have a chunky compote. Set aside while you make the zabaglione.

Put a saucepan with a little water over a high heat until the water is boiling.

Meanwhile, put the egg yolks in a heatproof bowl (such as a Pyrex glass bowl) and add the Marsala and sugar. Place the bowl over the pan of hot water and turn the heat down to low so that the water is just simmering. Using an electric hand whisk, whisk the egg mixture over the hot pan for a good 5–10 minutes, until it is thick and fluffy and the mixture will hold a 'W' on the top of the bowl when drawn with the beaters. Remove the pan from the heat and continue to whisk until the mixture has cooled to room temperature.

Divide the dark fruit compote evenly between the serving dishes – it will still be a little warm, and this is fine – then spoon the zabaglione over the top and serve straight away.

Freezer adaptation:

If you can't find frozen blackcurrants, supermarkets often do bags of 'forest fruit' or 'dark fruit' mixtures, which are also delicious in this. Just use 350g (12oz) of this mixture in place of the blackcurrants and cherries in the recipe above.

Will it re-freeze?

Nope, this is definitely one to serve fresh. Although you could arguably freeze the dark fruit compote if you have too much.

Serves 4
–
Prep 10 mins
–
Cook 20 mins

FREEZER STRAWBERRY JAM VE (AND A BAKED ALASKA TO USE IT IN)

I always baulk at the amount of sugar that goes into jam, but freezing your jam, instead of jarring it and storing at ambient temperature, means you can get away with adding much less sugar – and it tastes much fresher. Make a big batch and freeze in small portions to take out as you finish the previous one (it will keep for a few days in the fridge). You can use frozen strawberries for this.

For the freezer strawberry jam
700g (1lb 9oz) frozen (or fresh) strawberries
3 tbsp lemon juice (about 1 lemon)
100g (3½oz/½ cup) caster (superfine) sugar
1 × 8g (¼oz) sachet pectin

For the baked Alaska
a ready-baked madeira loaf cake
1 × 500ml (17fl oz) tub vanilla ice cream (in a rough rectangular shape)
4 large egg whites
250g (9oz/1¼ cups) caster (superfine) sugar

Freezer adaptation:
You could use any berries you find in the freezer for the jam – in fact, a mixture might be delicious, and it's a great way to use up the odds and ends of bags. Experiment!

Will it re-freeze?
Yes, that's the point of it! (Although, don't try to freeze the baked Alaska – that won't work.)

Makes 500ml
–
Prep 5 mins
–
Cook 20 mins

For the jam, put the berries in a large saucepan with the lemon juice and cook over a low–medium heat, stirring regularly, until the berries have broken down and the mixture has thickened. Add the sugar and pectin and stir continuously until the sugar has dissolved. Increase the heat to medium–high and boil for 4 minutes, then turn off the heat. Do a quick set test – put a little jam on a cold plate and leave it for 30 seconds or so. Push it with your finger and if it wrinkles, it has reached setting point and is ready. If not, cook a little bit longer then test again. Once setting, leave it to cool, then portion into small freezer tubs and freeze until needed. (Note: it will be a slightly softer set than normal jam.)

To make the baked Alaska, preheat the oven to 220°C/425°F/gas mark 7.

Slice the curved top off the Madeira loaf cake so that you are left with a flat, brick-shaped piece of cake. Using an apple corer, bore holes into the cake and remove the cores – about 5 or 6 should do it – being careful not to go all the way down, so there is still a layer of cake at the base. Fill these holes with strawberry jam, then spread jam over the top of the cake, too.

Turn the ice cream out of the tub (you may need to dunk it in a sink of hot water to melt it around the sides to release it) and trim it down so that it is the same size as the cake. Place it on top of the cake and place the whole thing in the freezer to get really cold while you prepare the meringue.

Put the egg whites in the bowl of a stand mixer (or use a mixing bowl and an electric hand mixer) and whisk until they are at soft, frothy peaks. Start adding the sugar, a little at a time, whisking well between each addition. Once all the sugar is added, whisk for at least 5 minutes longer until you have a firm and glossy meringue.

Remove the cake and ice cream block from the freezer and spread the meringue generously over the whole mound of cake and ice cream. Bake for 3–4 minutes until lightly golden, then serve immediately.

BERRIES & GIN

There's an amazing affinity between gin and berries, so if you've got a bottle of Gordon's gathering dust and a couple of bags of berries in the freezer, these two won't disappoint – both a twist on a classic drink, but more fruity than their originals. Both cocktails serve one, but the syrup or purée will run to a few more.

Clover Club v

For the syrup
150g (5½oz) frozen raspberries
about 70g (2½oz) caster (superfine) sugar (see method)

For the cocktail
60ml (2fl oz/4 tbsp) gin
15ml (½fl oz/1 tbsp) raspberry syrup (see above)
15ml (½fl oz/1 tbsp) lemon juice
ice cubes, for shaking
15ml (½fl oz/1 tbsp) egg white
freeze-dried raspberries, to decorate

Very Berry Bramble VE

For the purée
100g (3½oz) frozen blackberries
20g (⅔oz) caster (superfine) sugar

For the cocktail
15ml (½fl oz/1 tbsp) blackberry purée
crushed ice, for the glass
45ml (1½fl oz/3 tbsp) gin
30ml (1fl oz/2 tbsp) lemon juice
15ml (½fl oz/1 tbsp) crème de mûre
2 fresh blackberries, to decorate

> Serves 1
> –
> Prep 10 mins
> –
> Cook 10 mins

Clover Club

To make the syrup, put the raspberries in a saucepan with 2 tbsp water and cook over gentle heat for about 8 minutes, or until the raspberries have broken down. Tip the contents of the pan into a fine-meshed sieve over a measuring jug and strain. You can gently move the berry mush about a little with a spoon to release more liquid, but don't press it through or the syrup with be cloudy. See how much liquid you have and add the same quantity of sugar (for example, if you have 70ml (2½fl oz) of liquid, add 70g (2½oz) of sugar). Rinse the pan, return the mixture to it and stir over a gentle heat until the sugar has dissolved, then leave to cool.

To make the cocktail, put the gin, raspberry syrup and lemon juice in a cocktail shaker with the ice and shake until a frost appears on the outside of the shaker and the liquid is very cold. Using tongs (or such), remove the ice cubes from the shaker and add the egg white. Shake vigorously until the egg white has frothed up and pour into a chilled coupe glass. Garnish with a sprinkling of freeze-dried raspberries.

Very Berry Bramble

To make the purée, put the blackberries and sugar in a pan with 1 tbsp water and cook over gentle heat for 8 minutes, or until the blackberries have broken down. Tip the mixture into a fine-meshed sieve and press it through with a spoon – you should have a thick purée. Leave to cool, then chill.

To make the cocktail, add the blackberry purée to a rocks glass, then fill the rest of the glass with crushed ice. Build the cocktail in the glass, first adding the gin, then the lemon juice, then drizzle the crème de mûre over the top. Garnish with fresh blackberries and serve.

Will it re-freeze?

The syrup and purée will freeze, but they don't make much and will both keep for a few days in the fridge anyway. Any cocktails should be made fresh.

INDEX